Learning Volume 2: Wake up Your Sleepy Conscience. The Art of Learning to Accept Reality and Choosing How to Live It.

LEARNING, Volume 2

Ana María Pepi

Published by Ana María Pepi, 2024.

LEARNING VOLUME 2: WAKE UP YOUR SLEEPY CONSCIENCE. THE ART OF LEARNING TO ACCEPT REALITY AND CHOOSING HOW TO LIVE IT.

First edition. March 20, 2024.

Copyright © 2024 Ana María Pepi.

ISBN: 979-8224420025

Written by Ana María Pepi.

Table of Contents

LEARNING

VOLUME 2

WAKE UP YOUR SLEEPY CONSCIENCE

The Art of Learning to Accept Reality
and Choosing How to Live it

Ana María Pepi

Discover other titles by **<u>Ana María Pepi</u>**:
LEARNING Volume 1: ABSOLUTE POWER.
The Art of Learning How to Do it.

Best
Seller

I invite you to visit my social networks:
Facebook: Aprendiendo

Instragram:_@aprendiendo999

Twitter:_AnaMariaPepi2

YouTube: @aprendiendo999

❤This book Is dedicated to my dear friend Rita Tidei❤
6/11/1967 - 16/03/2023

Farewell Prayer

by **Gerardo Schmedling**

Thank you for everything we shared, for all the happy moments, and for everything we learned together.

You don't have to do anything more here. Your role in this world has ended. You can leave in peace because you've done everything you needed to do... and you always did your best; nothing remains unfinished. Now, other people will take care of the material activities you once handled, ensuring they continue to function smoothly.

Continue on your path to the wonderful world of light that awaits you. Don't look back, don't look down, only look up. Seek the light that guides you to your Father's dwelling.

Fill yourself with happiness and take the loving hands of your brothers who have come to receive you. See their happy, radiant faces as they welcome your arrival. They were waiting for you and now receive you with boundless joy.

Fully embrace your new world and rejoice in the presence of your teachers. You are now embarking on an experience of peace, love, and appreciation for everything you have understood.

~~~~~~~

"The friends we lose do not rest on earth... they are buried in our heart"
Alexandre Dumas, The Count of Monte Cristo, 1845.
~~~~~~~

Acknowledgments

I thank God for everything I have. I recognize and accept life's tough situations as opportunities to learn from them, strengthen my life energy, and take action. Gratitude turns problems into blessings.

I'm grateful for the spiritual teachers whose writings have helped and guided me on this path of personal growth and spiritual evolution. Their names are shared inside the book.

I'm thankful for my readers because they are also my teachers, and I'm the student. Learning something new every day allows me to, in turn, contribute by sharing my own transformation journey in these pages. This way, it gets recorded in the universal cosmic library that belongs to all of humanity: The Akashic Records, which take place in the realm of the spiritual. I'd like to give you a sneak peek that it will be the next level I'll be discussing in my upcoming book, **"LEARNING Volume 3"**.

Introduction

What did we come to LEARN in this LIFE?

To read this book, you don't need to believe in anything, I won't be talking about religion, politics, or anything like that. It's about embarking on a spiritual journey inward. It's time to take a peek inside ourselves and connect with who we are, to get to know ourselves better and learn from the experiences we collect along this temporary path called **LIFE.**

"LIFE IS A MARVELOUS OPPORTUNITY TO LEARN HOW TO BE HAPPY AND LEARN HOW TO LOVE."

Gerardo Schmedling[1]

Based on the teachings of this magnificent **master**, with his **Science of ACCEPTOLOGY** and author of the **"SCHOOL OF MAGIC LOVE"**, I wholeheartedly thank him for guiding me on my transformation journey. He used to say:

"Life is a Perfect part of the Order of the Universe, and you don't need to change a thing about it." "As long as you want to change anything about what's happening around you, it's because you don't accept it. If you don't accept it, it's because you don't see it as it is."

Open up and let the Vital Energy of the Universe fill you with Inner Light.

That's what's called AWAKENING!

In **A Course in Miracles**[2], **Jesus of Nazareth**, the spiritual master who marked a before and after of his existence, tells us that... **"what you teach, you will learn."**

But... **There is no one to teach but oneself!**

That is why, with the simplest possible language, I am writing this **LEARNING saga...** because they say that **by teaching you learn twice** and every day we have something new to learn.

Living is learning, and an ideal way to learn is to teach what one knows, to expand it into new forms of relating to the **Unity of the Creator**. In this sense spiritual learning is highly creative.

I'm not trying to convince or teach anyone anything, as my reader is my teacher, and I am the student on this journey toward wisdom.

For Socrates, with the famous phrase "[...] **I only know that I know nothing", wisdom comes precisely from the recognition of one's own ignorance.**

When you understand that the OTHER person you relate to is your MIRROR, then they become your TEACHER to learn about YOURSELF...

"After all, I'm never sure that the criticisms of others are meant for me. Maybe when you criticize me, you're actually criticizing the parts of me that are just like the parts of yourself you don't like... That makes sense, right?" , Jorge Bucay.[3]

Always remember that relationships with other people are very important for introspection, for getting to know ourselves, and for uncovering truths deep within our being.

Everyone always has something to teach us, whether to help us grow and evolve or simply to inform us about something.

That's why it's no coincidence that we've crossed paths with them.

Every single being has something to GIVE, every single being has something to RECEIVE or NEED TO KNOW....

BE A RECEIVER OF LOVE, ENERGY AND TRANSFORMATION

Try to maintain **good interpersonal relationships with everyone** because it's good for your health, and you'll live a happier life.

Only **Consciousness in Love** can definitely liberate the human being who has chosen to live in suffering and dependence on external factors in order to achieve happiness and live in peace every moment of their life.

We need to become aware that we CANNOT change the events of our lives, but we CAN CHOOSE how to experience them.

"We are the decisions we make." – Patrick Ness[4]

Frequently, our decisions are influenced by the narratives we construct about the outcomes of our future actions.

In "A Monster Calls"[5], a 2016 dark fantasy drama film directed by J. A. Bayona from a screenplay by Patrick Ness and based on Ness' 2011 novel of the same name. It stars Liam Neeson, Sigourney Weaver, Felicity Jones, Toby Kebbell and Lewis MacDougall. In the film, Conor O'Malley (MacDougall) grapples with his mother's terminal illness (cancer) as he is visited by the Monster (Neeson), a giant anthropomorphic yee tree who tells him stories. The Monster says to Connor:

"Your mind will believe the compassionate lies, but it also knows the painful truths that make those lies necessary. And your mind will punish you for believing both."

Psychologist Jorge Bucay makes us reflect on the topic of choice[6].

"Everyone constructs their life by choosing their path. [...] Is the chosen path always the right one? Rightness lies in the choice, not in the outcome. The path sets a direction, and a direction is much more than a result. [...] You choose where and decide until when because your path is exclusively your own. [...] What is the purpose of your life? Why do I live? Not why, but for what. Not how, but for what. Not with whom, but for what. Not about what, but for what. The question is personal. It's about YOUR LIFE. What is the purpose of your life? Answering this question sincerely is finding the compass for the journey. [...] Not knowing how to answer it or dismissing this question can be a way of expressing the decision to remain lost. [...] Discovering the purpose of your life is finding the key to happiness."

In A Course in Miracles, it is stated:

"You might believe that you are responsible for what you do, but not for what you think. The truth is that you are responsible for what you think because it is only at this level that you can exercise your power of choice. Your actions are the result of your thoughts. You cannot separate truth from the behavior by granting autonomy to the latter."

While in the J. A. Bayonas's film, "A Monster Calls" (2016), the Monster tells Connor:

"You don't write your life with words [...] You write it with actions. What you think is not important. The only important thing is what you DO".[...] The important thing is to tell the TRUTH...[7]

Anthony de Mello, on the other hand, tells us, "**Thought can organize the world so well that you are able to see it.**"

And according to **Jorge Bucay, "Desire makes sense when I can transform it into an action".**

Therefore, **I deeply believe that thoughts create our ideal world, but to make it a reality, we must take action.**

We are responsible for both these actions because we have the power to **CHOOSE** what, with what **attitude**, and when to do it. **As for how, we leave it in the hands of the Universe**, which, through a series of synchronicities and our intuition, will guide us on the means to achieve it.

The important thing is to take the first step.

In my first book in the series, **LEARNING: "Absolute Power". The Art of Learning How to Do it,** we took that first step in the physical realm by focusing on knowledge about our brain and everything that results from its proper functioning for good life outcomes. The spiritual or metaphysical realm played a more introductory role, to be explored in depth in this second book, which is entirely dedicated to it.

"Metaphysical means beyond the physical, in other words, the science that studies and deals with everything that is invisible to our physical senses. It gives purpose to everything we don't understand, everything mysterious, everything that lacks an obvious explanation. And it is precise", as **Conny Mendez** said.

And here, I present to you the continuation of the **LEARNING** series, Volume 2: "Wake up your Sleepy Conscience". The Art of Learning to Accept Reality and Choose How to Live It.

To connect with the Non-Local Consciousness or Supraconsciousness, we must ascend to the next level, which exists in the **spiritual or metaphysical realm.** In this invisible dimension, **I have attempted to find explanations** for various concepts to address many of the **existential questions** that humans constantly ask themselves:

Where do we come from?
What are we made of?
Does God exist?
What did we come to do in this world?

Where do we go after physical death?

What must we do (or not do) to change situations that don't work?

Today, thanks to quantum physics, these questions can have scientific answers. They can be explained and verified scientifically, serving as support and help to compensate for everything that the scientific method or theoretical physics cannot explain. Even if we don't believe it, **everything has a scientific explanation, even the existence of God.**

In this second book, **"Wake up your Sleepy Conscience"**, we will continue the journey of transformation and growth that we began together in the first book of the series: **LEARNING how to put your Absolute Power into practice, how to become new and improved individuals, and how to achieve the results you have set for yourself in life, whether in the areas of money, health, or love.**

Starting with the premise that a human being is made of a body in the physical realm and a soul in the spiritual realm, we reach the conclusion that there is no success without putting **EMOTION** into the things we undertake each day.

EMOTION originates in the **HEART**, where **EVERYTHING in creation begins!**

The core concept from the first book of the **LEARNING** series is that the **MIND CAN DO ANYTHING WITH ITS ABSOLUTE POWER.**

Matter cannot think or feel; it merely reflects your emotional state.

It is your beliefs that create your material world.

If you believe it, you create it!

For a thought to become a physical reality, a belief is necessary. But be cautious of limiting beliefs—those born from the Ego that always attempt to keep you in your comfort zone and can become your very own prison!

The **MIND** is the brain in action!

The **brain** is a **supercomputer**, and our thoughts and beliefs are the **language, the application program,** to achieve all the **results** we want. Therefore, **the brain is the decoder of our thoughts.**

The brain is the Golden Gate that allows us to think, learn, activate the heart to create and experience emotion, evolution, innovation, and growth. In other words, it connects us to a new dimension where we can have a deeper and more successful life experience.

But the MIND is not only in the brain...

The MIND exists everywhere.

The MIND is omnipresent because it exists in another dimension, more subtle than the 3D reality to which the human being belongs.

Indeed, it is in the third dimension, in this realm, where the true spiritual-evolutionary journey begins. Each soul is put to the test on a long voyage we call Life. And when you find yourself confused, all you need is a teacher, a guide to show you where you lost your way.

Humans are all interacting in a continuous process of growth and evolution. We are like children who are part of a great universal or cosmic school, where we are learning with every step we take, with every experience we live, to recognize the vast potential of wisdom within our being. This means that through our firsthand experiences, our understanding of reality is defined. We begin to awaken our consciousness and understand that everything that exists and happens in our lives has a deeper meaning beyond the simple surface of things that surround us.

Finally, we understand that there are laws that govern the universal order and all our experiences. Our own **BEING** must go through a path of evolution and transformation that brings us increasingly closer to our deeper consciousness to understand that **WE ARE ALL ONE, and we are ALL INTERCONNECTED!**

"Once upon a time, there was a fish that asked an older one where it could find the ocean... The older fish replied, 'The ocean? You're in it right now!' To which the first fish responded, 'This is water, what I want is the ocean.'" — Anthony de Mello.

Sometimes we do not realize that the **fullness of life we are looking for is already in our present**, which is the **here and now**. Our expectations close our eyes and heart and do not allow us to see and live **in the present moment**, where **everything is possible**.

We are already in that place we desire and seek so much. And what's more... what we are looking for is within ourselves. We are at ONE with the Almighty!

Therefore, **STOP SEEKING**...Open your eyes and See. **You already have it ALL AROUND YOU!**

Be Open to Receive...

"The greatest learning of the age lies in ACCEPTING life exactly as it comes to us. To be GRATEFUL for what we have is something many of us learn as the years go by", Anthony de Mello.

Being humble leads you to look at the world with surprise and this is one of the most beautiful immediate characteristics of **children:** to be always amazed by new things and to live every day as something extraordinary and surprising.

When we, adults, become humble like children, we return to live a full life and to rejoice in the simple and pleasant things of every day.

We must learn to be more and more like children!

We learn that we all pass through this world to be happy, but... we cannot take charge of the happiness of others, nor can we expect someone else to provide it for us.

Our mission in this life is to give ourselves the possibility to be HAPPY because we DESERVE it, by the simple fact of EXISTING...

Each of us is responsible for making ourselves happy, and this depends purely on **our ability to accept and appreciate, without pretending to change, the people, situations, difficulties and events that are present in our lives.**

"Difficulties then reveal themselves to us as positive stages of life, since indeed they are the ones that allow us to reach happiness.

"Difficulties are an integral part of the path of love"; Jorge Bucay, "The Way to Happiness", 2004.

Happiness has to do with what happens inside us and not on the outside.

Happiness and unhappiness are in the being, not in what surrounds it.

That is why if we do not like something about a situation or someone, we have to start changing ourselves inside and then it will be reflected, by law of correspondence, outside.

Happiness is a natural condition of the human being.

He who does not make himself happy is a danger to humanity. The **ego** will always lead us to put ourselves in the position of **victims** and **look for people to blame who deserve to be punished.**

This is the beginning of all conflict among men.

To be happy we have to understand that everything that happens to us in life is for our good and it is necessary to learn what we do not know yet, for example:

Learning to listen, respect and accept others with their beliefs, tastes and individual decisions.

Learning that everyone and no one is right, because we all have different lenses[8] **to interpret and understand life, and that being observers of reality, we are co-creators with the Universe.**

Learning that there is no one to blame, because everyone does the best they can with the best they know and each is 100% responsible for their own decisions.

Learning that it is necessary to make mistakes in order to evolve. Indeed, being wrong is a sacred right that we fail to understand and therefore many, for fear of being wrong, cling to their beliefs of knowledge.

He who believes in his knowledge, is incapable of opening himself to learn more about what, by its results, shows that he still does not know.

"He who does not dare to come down from the pedestal of believing he knows everything, can learn nothing from others, whom without listening he despises because he assumes or, even worse, decides that they can teach him nothing". [9] **Jorge Bucay.**

"Fear is the non-acceptance of what has not yet happened, while suffering is the non-acceptance of what has already happened".

"Everyone has what is necessary to be happy,
but few are able to be happy with what they have"
Gerardo Schmedling.

"He who is not happy with little, will not be happy with much", Lao Tse.

CHAPTER 1

THE BEGINNING OF EVERYTHING
THE WHOLE UNIVERSE IS ENERGY
WE ARE ALL INTERCONNECTED

As I said before that everything has a scientific explanation, it is appropriate to identify the **two types of physics** that, through the ages, have been explaining to us the concepts of existence:

1) Theoretical physics or scientific method: it is a realistic science, it is based on natural laws, objective, materialistic, causalistic, limiting, deterministic, it is based on a concept of linear time: past-present-future, i.e. a temporally limited concept.

2) Quantum physics: it is a subjective, extrasensory science, based on pure energy or electromagnetic waves in constant motion, time is circular, it is the same eternity of the present, where everything is probability, indeterminacy, uncertainty. Quantum fields are intertwined: fluctuations at one point tend to coincide with fluctuations at another point.

Therefore, there is a transfer of information independent of space and time that pervades each field with a minimal amount of energy, in its fundamental state, known as zero-point energy. (**Masahiro Hotta** in 2008, and 15 years later, **Kazuki Ikeda**, demonstrated that quantum teleportation of energy was possible. And today it can be incorporated into the emerging quantum Internet).

At a certain point in history, it was conceived that there was an incompatibility in the theoretical scientific world because it could not explain the activities of the mind, with the natural laws of the materialistic world, because the mind has no material substratum.

Therefore, theoretical scientists admitted that there was an abyss that they could not explain and left it in the hands of **quantum physics, which is based on the concept that the whole Universe is energy, that the whole Universe is interconnected** and that **we, human beings, are stardust.**

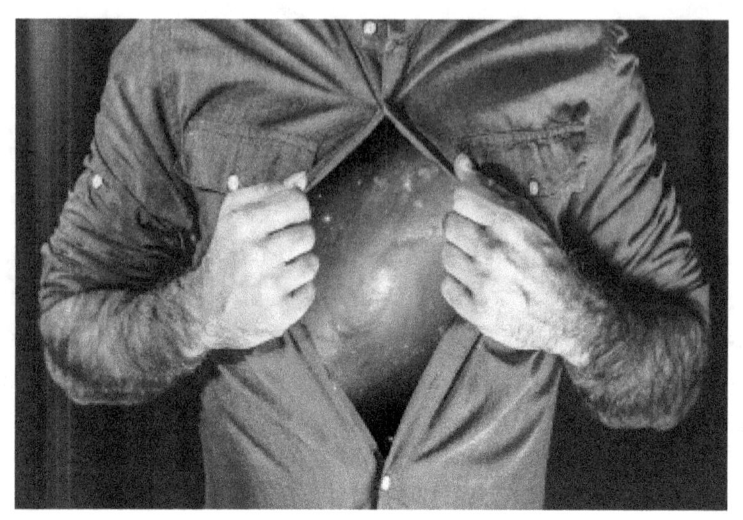

What Are We Made of?

The scientific method considers the human being, from the anthropological point of view, as body or matter and as mind or epiphenomenon, i.e. the consequence of the metabolic activity of matter, which is the brain.

On the other hand, for quantum physics or metaphysics, all those mental activities, which are thoughts, consciousness, memory, feelings, emotions, have been studied in depth as the psychic activities of the human being. For quantum physics, **THE HUMAN BEING** is neither body nor mind, but is **PURE CONSCIOUSNESS.**

WE ARE PURE ENERGY !

If the scientific method considers the mind as an epiphenomenon, that is, if all mental activity depends on metabolic or neuronal activity, then the famous phrase of the French theoretical physicist, mathematician and philosopher, **René Descartes**, spontaneously comes to mind: "[...] **I think, therefore I am**", (Discourse on Method, 1637). But, **this reasoning is limited because it means that if I stop thinking, with brain death, then I cease to exist!**

Since for conventional medicine clinical death is verified by brain death and this reasoning comes through the scientific method, that is why we deduce that the latter is limiting and deterministic.

Then, how can we explain the existence of all those transcendental phenomena, such as paranormal phenomena, telepathy, clairvoyance, precognition, near-death experiences (NDE), mystical experiences, reincarnation and many others?

These are all psychic phenomena, which have to do with something that we do not see, but that exists, such as life after death.

We have to look for these types of answers in other disciplines such as quantum physics or dynamics, which, in fact, can scientifically explain to us how all that which we cannot see with our human sensory organs works.

What Does Quantum Mean?

Related to quanta or units of energy; elementary particle associated with a field of forces: quantum mechanics. The theory formulated by the German physicist **Max Planck,** according to which the emission and absorption of energy do not take place in continuous processes, in a bound state, but at intervals to each of which corresponds **the emission or absorption of an elementary unit of energy, which implies the existence of minimal packets of energy called quanta.**

When **Max Planck** received the **Nobel Prize in 1900**, he said, shaking the physical foundations of his time: **"There is no matter as such! All matter originates and exists only by virtue of a force. We must assume behind this force the existence of an Intelligent and Conscious Mind. This Mind is the Matrix of all matter".**

Quantum physics is based on the foundation that the **WHOLE UNIVERSE IS ENERGY** and has scientific validity because the results are explained and demonstrated mathematically or with experiments carried out in a laboratory.

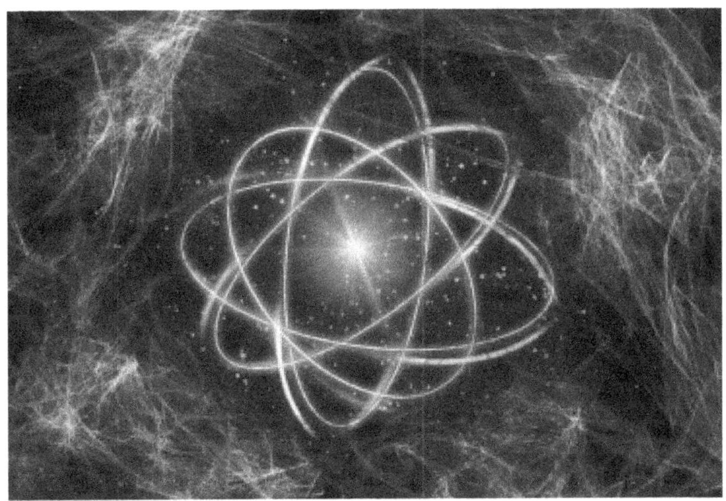

Quantum physics was born thanks to the New Zealander and physicist, **Ernest Rutherford**, who, with his discovery of the atomic nucleus in 1911, formulated the knowledge of the **structure of the atom**: a basic unit formed by a very dense central nucleus, with nucleons, containing its protons and neutrons(+), and a series of electrons(-) revolving around it. These particles are grouped in different numbers to form the chemical elements (oxygen, carbon, etc.), but they will always be distributed according to a **fixed structure.** That is to say, we can have different types of atoms (the hydrogen atom, the oxygen atom, etc.) but their **subatomic particles** are always organized in a similar way to a **planetary system.**

The atom is the most basic unit or fundamental component of all matter.

Everything that exists in the physical, material, known Universe is made of atoms. The whole Universe, all the stars, galaxies, planets and other celestial bodies, plants, animals, this very book, your laptop or cell phone, the table where you eat your lunch, and **we ourselves** too, like every living creature, **are made of atoms.**

Atoms are grouped together to form molecules, and these molecules constitute all the materials we know with the physical and chemical characteristics we observe. Every observed object is nothing more than an organized set of molecules, atoms and electrons that rotate around each other at an inconceivable speed.

Therefore, **every particle of physical matter is in a state of continuous, highly agitated motion.**

Nothing is ever still and although it may appear to the motionless physical eye, there is no solid physical matter, such as a piece of steel, that does not have molecules, atoms and electrons whirling around it and are of the same nature and moving at the same speed as the electrons of gold, silver, tin.

Besides, everything solid is empty. We can explain this by taking as an example our body which is made of atoms.

Let's think about the metaphor of the body which is made up of organs; the organs by tissues; the tissues by cells; the cells by molecules and the molecules by atoms; the atoms by quarks. But without going further in depth where only experts can go, they explain in general terms that **quarks**, the most elementary particles of the Universe, together with electrons, gluons, neutrinos and photons **are pure energy** and from there we deduce that our body is energy.

The experts explain in simple words that what makes up a proton (quarks and gluons) represent **only 1% of its mass, the other 99% is energy!**

It is therefore simpler to think of these particles as a presence in a particle field that permeates the entire Universe.

For quantum mechanics, energy is electromagnetic waves vibrating at a high degree of frequency, that is, with a high degree of vibration.

Therefore, the solid is empty, just as the whole Universe is interconnected because it is and we are pure energy with it and in it.

A quantum physicist would give us an example of this type: imagine that one of your atoms is a golf ball and you put it in the center of a stadium or soccer field, do you know where the electrons are spinning.in the last row of the seats of the stadium!

So, now we know that there is a lot of empty space in our body. That means that you can pass through bodies. If you have seen **the film "Ghost"**, you can already get an idea...

This can only be explained by quantum physics, because it is in a high-frequency energy wave state and that is how you can pass through particles, that is to say that everything solid is empty.

Quantum physics is based on the fundamental element of the Universe, which is not material but energy and its conservation principle:

ENERGY is neither created nor destroyed,

IT TRANSFORMS

ENERGY endures ETERNALLY.

Energy is in continuous motion, in a vibratory state that propagates in electromagnetic waves with a variable amplitude (or frequency) and height (or intensity).

The French physicist **Louis V. de Broglie**, in 1924, showed us that **energy could be unfolded** and **presented either as energy, which were electromagnetic waves, or as matter, i.e. particles.**

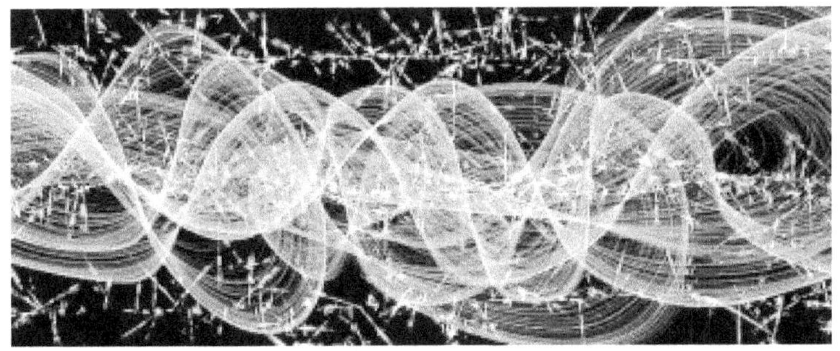

The first convincing demonstration of this was found in the laboratory with the **double-slit experiment**, carried out by **Richard Feynman** in 1965, a variant of **Thomas Young**'s experiment that, in 1801, had demonstrated the wave motion of light.

Because **it demonstrates the fundamental limitation of the observer's ability to predict experimental results, Richard Feynman said: "this experiment has in it, the heart and only mystery of quantum mechanics".**

From him was born the concept known as the **Observer Principle: if a flow of electrons is propagated through a double slit, it was seen that electromagnetic waves could be observed, but, at the moment when an observer intervened, that flow of electrons was also propagated as particles**, in other words, **it was transformed into matter.**

That is to say that this same energy could be made to collapse, thanks to the presence of an INTELLIGENT CONSCIOUSNESS, into matter.

Thanks to this discovery of **QUANTUM PHYSICS**, with the experiment of the **OBSERVER EFFECT**, today we know that we are no longer only observers of the Universe, (as stipulated by the limiting scientific method, based only on the laws of nature that could not be modified), but... **WE ARE CO-CREATORS OF THE UNIVERSE!**

Jesus of Nazareth said, "You are gods but you have forgotten..."

Our mind can also create or modify molecular reality, because it has an absolute power that comes from the heart and, through emotion, vibrates in the quantum field.

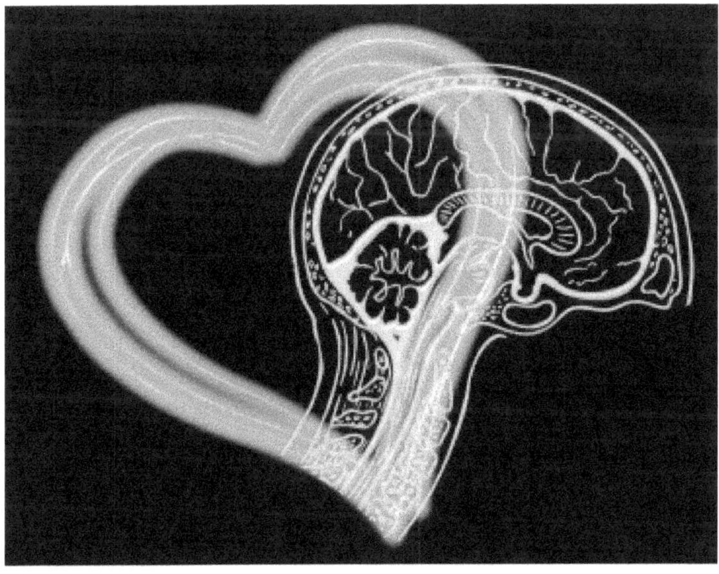

This could be proven thanks to the amazing experiments of the Japanese scientist **Masaru Emoto**, who photographed frozen water molecules, opening an incredible door to the possibility that our mind is capable of creating Reality.

Emoto photographed molecules from polluted and spring waters. What he discovered was that **pure water created crystals of incredible beauty, while dirty water created only chaos.**

Then, he proceeded to place labels with **words like Love or Hate,** finding a similar effect: **love provoked beautiful molecular shapes, while hate generated chaos.**

Finally, he tried placing **relaxing music, folk music and thrash metal music,** with the **contrasting result between beauty and chaos** that could be seen in the photographs.

If we take into account that **80% of our body is water,** we will understand how **our emotions, our words and even the music we listen to, influence our reality to be more or less harmonious.**

Our internal structure is reacting to all external influences, reorganizing the atoms of the molecules.

The biological explanation to this phenomenon is that **the atoms that compose the molecules** (in this case, the two of Hydrogen and one of Oxygen) **can be arranged in different ways: harmoniously or chaotically, depending on the resonance that I transmit to them with my emotional vibration.**

How was the Universe created?

Thanks to advances in **quantum physics**, today, not only can we understand how the Universe originated, but also, with the measurement of time through the atomic clock or optical lattice clock, we know the age of the Universe with this formula 14×10^9 years!

Fourteen billion years ago there was a huge **concentration of energy and that energy collapsed into matter,** with the cosmological model of the **BIG BANG** and the Universe we know today was created and we know it is still expanding, thanks to the **Hubble space telescope (1990)** and the new **James Webb telescope (2022)**, with unprecedented resolution and sensitivity.

But **for energy to collapse into matter, there had to be a PRIMARY INTELLIGENCE or PRIMORDIAL BEING which is GOD, or whatever you want to call it, the Creator of the Universe.**

That is to say that the **WHOLE**, which was pure **ENERGY, GOD or PRIMARY INTELLIGENCE, collapsed it into MATTER.**

Each one can give the name he wants to that **PRIMARY INTELLIGENCE or PRIMORDIAL BEING**, which is **UNIQUE for ALL**. It is not necessary to belong to a religion to understand this concept.

When **Einstein** was asked if **he believed in God**, he said he believed in the **Perfect Universe which is governed by laws established by a Primary Intelligence which is God.**

God is the First Cause, he is the Creator of EVERYTHING.

With the **origin of religions**, each one of them has given a **different name** to the same and **unique First Cause or Creator of EVERYTHING**:

God, Universe, The Father, The Divine Source, Jehovah, Allah, Brahman, Tao, etc,.

If we want to give a name to this consciousness of ours that endures through time and space, it is the SUPRACONSCIOUSNESS or NON-LOCAL CONSCIOUSNESS, which is above the cerebral or neuronal consciousness.

Moreover, we can say that this **SUPRACONSCIOUSNESS is HOLISTIC** with respect to the First Energy.

As well as it was demonstrated that a **fractal** is a **WHOLE**, a **total hologram**, formed by **multiple parts or fractions** with the particularity that **each one of the parts has the structure and properties of the whole,** hence our consciousness is holistic and has three properties:

1) It is Omnipresent: because it is eternal, where time is circular. It exists only in the here and now, that is, in the **PRESENT time**. It is a subtle energy.

2) It is Omniscient: it knows everything and is everywhere, beyond what we see or can grasp with our senses. In other words, it is outside the brain; it is a Non Local Consciousness and manifests itself through intuition that always tells us the truth.

3) It is Omnipotent: it can do everything.

Does God Exist?

Scientifically, it has been possible to verify the existence of God thanks to the theoretical physicist, **Michu Kaku**, who carried out an experiment with subatomic particles, called tachyons, taking them to an extraordinary speed, close to the speed of light, in a particle accelerator, thanks to which he was able to verify that: they could not be influenced by any external force because they behaved according to their own essence.

They had a **PERFECT ORDER!**

If there is a perfect order, there are laws that govern it. If there are perfect laws governing the Universe, then there is a **FIRST INTELLIGENCE**, which is **GOD.**

Therefore, **GOD EXISTS.**

Reading "**The Spirit Book**" [10], we learn that:

"**God is the Supreme Loving Intelligence; the First Creator of all things. God is the expanded Consciousness full of supreme love capable of changing everything about life".[...] "To believe in God it is enough to look around you and admire the works of His Creation. The Universe Exists, therefore Everything has a Cause"." Rationally, it is not possible to admit an effect without a cause. To doubt the existence of God is to deny that every effect has a cause, and to advance that nothingness can do anything."**

"It is by the work that the Author is known."

You too are a work of God!

Allan Kardec

In substance, each of us, **human beings**, have this **First Energy within ourselves, it is the Supraconsciousness and it is holistic**, that is why we are told that **we are gods but, we do not know it or simply, we have forgotten it.** That is to say **that energy affects the whole Universe** and can be transformed into particles or matter and that is thanks to that **Intelligence, Energy, First Cause, God, who collapsed the energy into matter.** That energy manifests in all of us through the **Supraconsciousness**, which is above the neuronal, cerebral or mental consciousness, that is why it is also called **Non Local Consciousness because it lasts eternally outside the brain and continues after the death of the brain.** Even before Christ, Eastern philosophy said that Supraconsciousness is a finite experience of the infinite. Victor Hugo said that this eternally enduring Consciousness of ours is the presence of God in ourselves.

The first energy is the infinite, that is, the first energy manifests itself in each one of us.

In the Bible, **Jesus of Nazareth** said: **"You are the sons of God".**

"You are made in his image and likeness".

We are the first energy but, **that supraconscious mind, we cannot detect it with our sensitive and sensory organs because it is an energy of a certain frequency, very high, very subtle, eternal,** which is in the **5th dimension,** some call it the sky, where everything that exists is found, everything you can imagine already exists there.

In the **4th dimension**, we find the **subconscious mind**, that is, the **programs of beliefs, ideas and ancestral memory** that we bring with us when we are born;

While the human dimension of the **conscious mind** is the three-dimensional, or low frequency energy collapsed into matter. Our existential reality tells us that we are limited beings within a physical body.

We must know that, besides the **5th dimension**, there are many more dimensions of pure subtle energy, **Supraconsciousness or Non Local Consciousness**, which we cannot grasp with our sensory or sensitive organs, but we have evidence of the presence of their existence.

One of these proofs is the **INTUITION**, also known as the sixth sense, the third eye or the premonitions.

Let's think when faced with a problem we use an intellective, rational, neuronal activity and we reason with the prefrontal part of our brain. The highest brain activities occur in this area. But, one day without reasoning, when we surrender and let the Universe, the Supraconsciousness, enlighten us, is when **we find the solution, thanks to intuition, which always tells us the truth because it sees and knows everything, beyond our own senses.**

Intuition is the First Energy that resides in each of us and it is never wrong!

The more spiritual and conscious one is of possessing that primary energy or non-local consciousness, the more intuitive the person becomes.

Another manifestation is **CREATIVITY**. To create is to originate from nothing a work of art, which is unique and unrepeatable because it is the fruit of one's Primary Consciousness and is born at the moment when you connect with your Non-Local Consciousness through an artistic language, which can be painting, music, writing, architecture, etc.

Beethoven, for example, said that he did not create the Ninth Symphony but copied it from his Supraconscious Mind.

Gauguin said the same thing. To paint a picture, he had to close his eyes and he copied everything that he had there, inside himself. "I close my eyes in order to see". **Gauguin** painted from his imagination, simply because he connected with his Supraconsciousness.

That is why machines, or artificial consciousness, will not be able to create anything because creation can originate only from the connection with an Intelligent Consciousness.

Another proof of our connection with the Supraconsciousness are all those **TRANSCENDENTAL MANIFESTATIONS** such as: near-death experiences; painless, peaceful and harmonious dying experiences; telepathy; precognition; reincarnation; mystical experiences. These are proofs that all of us are a Non-Local Consciousness that endures after our death.

The Superconsciousness is governed by positive dynamic laws, of very high frequency, always vital, such as altruism, empathy, justice, kindness, forgiveness, compassion, love, and they move in a field of unity between me and the other, because we are all one.

"Love is the most powerful energy in the Universe," said Einstein.

Another proof of the existence of Supraconsciousness is the granting of FREE WILL.

We have the power of Choice.

We are 100% responsible for everything around us.

"I am responsible for the decisions I make, therefore, I am free to stay or leave, to say or shut up, to insist or to abandon, to take the risks I decide and to go out into the world to find what I need" [...]where... Freedom is the ability to choose within what is possible"; Jorge Bucay, "20 Steps Forward. "[11]

According to our consciousness, we can choose to be slaves of the ego which has four powers: ignorance, selfishness, materialism and fear of death above all things, and get caught up in the past or in the future. Otherwise, we can choose to follow the laws of Supraconsciousness or Non Local Consciousness which is the **ETERNAL TRUTH** to achieve **freedom**. We act with altruism, empathy, love, being conscious that we are part of a **whole. We are twinned with a whole and that makes us free.**

The only way to inhibit the ego is to **LIVE** in the **PRESENT,** because the ego is always clinging to the past: with feelings of guilt and remorse, of everything that has not been achieved in yesterday... Or it is projected into the future: with the feeling of anxiety, which creates the uncertainty of what is to come tomorrow, or that state of anguish, because you do not know if you will be able to achieve or not what you have set for yourself.

Instead, it is only in the **PRESENT** moment when you have **LIFE,** when you **EXIST** and have **PRESENCE.**

CHAPTER 2

EXISTENTIAL DIMENSIONS

Dimensions are the different states of consciousness that we experience on the path towards becoming the unique being, which is God. These are the evolutionary steps that the being chose to experience to return to the Divine source, to the Home.

All dimensional levels exist in the here and now. The difference lies in the wavelength. We all know that the third dimension is the world where us humans live. In physics, dimensions are related to the length, extension, and volume that a line, surface, or body will occupy in space. **We live on planet Earth, a "three-dimensional" world.** It is the most fundamental because we acquire almost all of our understanding about existence here through personal experiences. **It's the dimension of matter.**

There are other dimensions on a plane that we cannot see with our eyes. From a spiritual perspective, dimensions are not physical locations but frequencies within which we vibrate; they are similar to radio waves with their frequencies.

We could also say that they are levels or states of evolutionary consciousness in development. As the being evolves, it can move through these dimensions, from the most basic or material level to the most evolved or spiritual, reaching its full development.

Each dimension is a source of support and guidance for spiritual evolution. Each dimension is governed by a set of specific laws and principles to function in harmony with the frequency of that vibration. Changing dimensions means expanding our consciousness or how we perceive reality. Therefore, we may find ourselves moving through a more energetic reality that resembles the world of dreams and imagination.

Transcended human beings can remain in various states or levels of consciousness simultaneously because we are all multidimensional beings. **All beings and things**, with their differences and distinct properties, **are vibrational expressions of a spiritual essence.**

Where do we come from, where are we, and where are we going?

1. **The first dimension: Monadic microcosm.**

The first dimension is responsible for transforming energy into matter. It is the basic frequency of atoms and molecules, and therefore, it is the energy of the microcosm. **It is the vibrational frequency of DNA activation.** It operates at an elementary pinpoint level of consciousness. It knows how to move from one point to another. On a material level, this dimension is described as **a quantum field that transforms energy into matter**, and it is cyclically connected to the seventh dimension as the matrix of existence.

In the first dimension, there are tiny and imperceptible energetic substantial units called monads. These are like metaphysical atoms, holistically speaking, as they contain encoded information of the entire cosmos within them. **They vibrate at a very subtle frequency, and through them, Universal Consciousness or Intelligence, God, creates different worlds.**

By the law of correspondence, "as above, so below," we understand that each fractal unit is a reflection of the whole. Each dimension is a mirror of the one above. The microcosm reflects the macrocosm and vice versa.

Minerals and water vibrate at this frequency. While minerals represent the crystalline aspect of it and water is its liquid one. It is also found in the fluids and electrical currents of the human body. It activates the genetic code and energetically drives the cellular system.**

When applied to humans, we could say that we experience the first dimension during the pre-fetal stage. It's a phase of potentialities, with a cellular division program and functions maintenance. All dimensions function at all scales, and they are the same throughout the Universe.

2) The second dimension: The elemental world

The second dimension is where most animals and plants exist. It's also physical and propels biological identity. It's responsible for biodiversity and the energies that facilitate it, like the elemental forces of nature. This is the vibration that maintains unity among species, often referred to as the collective unconsciousness of species. It's how animals of the same species recognize each other for reproductive purposes.

In this dimension, consciousness is collective. Several beings share the same guiding consciousness, functioning automatically as a group for their evolution. Many animals act on instinct, even though they possess what we could call an infra-consciousness, a mind that is just beginning to mature. There is no individual differentiation or self-recognition in this level of consciousness. There is no temporal/spatial reference. Consciousness is linear and two-dimensional.

This vibrational frequency corresponds to the basic world of biological force driving life. Unicellular beings, plants, insects, and some animals are part of this bilinear consciousness state.

Our cells are a micro-reflection of ourselves. They possess their own consciousness but are unaware of themselves, synchronized with the rhythm of the second dimension. They function together in a predetermined manner, aiding the development of internal biology.

Bird flocks that migrate, swarms of bees, ant colonies, and even microscopic entities work simultaneously as if they were one single entity. They act cohesively as a whole, maintaining a mathematical distance between each other and only breaking formation when under attack.

Within this vibrational field of the second dimension are the energetic forces that govern the five elements (earth, water, fire, air, and ether). This dimension essentially governs the course of nature and evolution, establishing the fundamental basis for the third dimension. Using the metaphor of human development, we could compare the second dimension to the fetal stage. We float, at one with the environment, in a state of non-ego and without temporal/spatial reference.

3) The third dimension: The physical world

The third dimension is where us humans exist. Like the second dimension, it's also physical, with consciousness being volumetric and three-dimensional. Here, there's a linear perception of time and space, allowing us to remember the past and project into the future while staying in the present.

In this dimension, we become self-aware, develop the ego, and believe we're separate from the whole. It's based on polarity, the illusion of separation, the development of individual identity, and the loss of group consciousness.

In a children's radio program with my friend and fellow Chilean writer **Nelson Carrizo**[11], I had a conversation with **"Nelsito"**, who asked me about the difference between humans and animals. I initially responded that **humans were intelligent and had a soul.** But **Nelsito**, being a perceptive child, **argued that animals were intelligent too and suggested they might also have souls.**

Ultimately, I can clarify that I was talking about human intelligence. **Humans, as part of the whole and capable of connecting with Supraconsciousness or Universal Intelligence, are the only ones able to CREATE their own reality or world because they have individual differentiation and self-recognition, capacities that animals in the second dimension do not yet possess.**

Animals can be **intelligent** to the extent that they're **guided by universal instinct, helping them distinguish beings of their species for reproductive purposes; that's their mission.**

Regarding the **soul**, I'd like to explain the difference between individualized souls, like those of humans vibrating in the third dimension, which have self-awareness, and **group souls, like those of animals in the second dimension. Unlike humans, animals don't have the individualization of self yet.**

In fact, all individualized souls come from the evolutionary process of group souls. Those of us who have the privilege of enjoying the company and love of our beloved pets should know that animals have a group soul and are preparing to take the next step toward individualization in another form of life with self-awareness. As a result, humans have a great responsibility towards animals as their elder siblings, and we must contribute with our behavior, characterized by more love, respect, harmony, and a higher vibrational frequency. We are helping in the evolutionary process of group souls.

Unfortunately, humanity often acts out of ignorance and unconsciousness of its significant responsibility in this evolutionary process. Many people mistreat animals and exploit them, hindering the process with speciesist treatment, as if we, as humans, were superior...

There is a mental world within all the realms of nature. It's true that these mental aspects are rudimentary compared to the human mind, or when comparing a mineral to an animal, but there exists a mental plane in all of them. Trees transport water and nutrients through their roots. There is collaboration, assistance, and intelligence among them. Therefore, it's clear that there is a mind in all forms of mineral, plant, and animal life, each with varying levels of development and complexity. This mental plane represents the highest level that matter can reach in its development and can demonstrate through its connection with other evolving life forms that have developed a mental plane.

The pacts of love between souls involve analyzing the process of evolution of self-awareness in the human soul at the present moment and its interrelation with processes of higher and lower consciousness that occur in life, in nature, and also relate to Mother Earth and the solar system.

As **Max Scheler** pointed out in his work "**Man's Position in the Cosmos**" in 1928, "**...unlike other animals, humans can distinguish the idea of reality, the essence of existence, and thus imagine and conceive a world different from the environment in which they find themselves. Thus, they are also capable of mythically or logically formulating the idea of something or someone beyond nature, understood as the complex of visible entities and events. Taken to its highest degree of abstraction, the idea of a Supernatural Power coincides with that of God.**"

This dimension is where we perceive ourselves as more separated from the whole than in any other. Therefore, in the 3D, the unique being faces more challenges of integration and growth. For humans, this process begins around the second year of life. It's a crucial learning stage where the process of fragmentation begins. It's when a child starts to differentiate from its surroundings as an individual, express its desires, and form its ego.

In the third dimension, we experience a process of splitting the self. We create our personality or "ego" when our consciousness has developed self-perception. This stage is known as the individuation of the self. At this point, the individual transitions into the third state of consciousness, corresponding to the vibrational frequency of the material world. In fact, the physical world could be considered the first existential level. In various esoteric traditions, it is referred to as the first dimension because, besides being the densest energetically due to the amount of condensed vibration in matter, it's the abode of the self-aware being, one with an identity and a perception of the world around it.

As our consciousness expands further, we become capable of perceiving other aspects of reality beyond the material, and we transition to the fourth dimension, where emotions come into play. We open up to perceive feelings and thoughts, each with different clarity and intensity.

4_ The fourth dimension: the astral plane

The fourth dimension serves as a passage to the fifth dimension, where we begin to become aware that we are not just physical bodies. Experiences like déjà vu (already seen or lived) and synchronicities become repetitive and widespread. We notice many changes, both within and outside ourselves. There is an inclination to seek knowledge about spirituality, rather than religion, to distinguish between the two. A call from our inner selves to spend time with ourselves becomes apparent. Self-analysis and self-discovery are prominent in this transition to the fourth dimension. We also become aware of the changes happening outside ourselves, seeing that the climate is constantly changing, and the days are no longer as they used to be. Time no longer seems to suffice to accomplish what we once did. In this dimension, we perceive time in cyclical decades or spiral forms (the present). There exists a quantum field where all possibilities and alternatives present themselves simultaneously. This is the frequency of absolute synchronicity, empathy, and telepathy.

It is the last dimension where we experience a physical body composed of carbon-14 as a learning vehicle. In this frequency, we perceive multidimensionality and realize our responsibility as we become aware that each of our actions affects the whole. At the human level, there is a need to connect with groups, review our relationships, seek healing and growth through therapies. It is also responsible for the breakdown of our physical structures, long-established economic and political beliefs that no longer align with this new vibration. We will continue to see and experience changes at all levels that do not correspond to the new energy, as the dimensional shift affects all scales. It's not a change that happens overnight but through gradual layers of consciousness.

Accepting the consciousness of the fourth dimension is what is called the Quantum Leap, and it is the most challenging step of the dimensional shift, as it involves profound changes in beliefs. Within this fourth dimension lies the so-called dream world. More than 80% of the time when you dream, you are actually visiting the astral plane. When your body falls asleep, the soul involuntarily leaves the body and travels to the astral plane or the fourth dimension. It's a vibrational frequency where consciousness navigates freely without constraints. In the same way, when a person passes away, their consciousness moves to the fourth dimension, crossing a light at the end of a tunnel.

This threshold has been described by millions of people who have experienced close encounters with death (NDEs). The afterlife, as many know it, corresponds to a parallel world called the astral plane.

This plane is divided into two main zones: the lower astral, where beings of very low vibration dwell: dark entities, demons, evil spirits, etcetera. Also called the underworld or hell by popular culture. While the high astral is where beings of high vibration such as awakened souls, elementals or nature spirits live: fairy elves, gnomes, salamanders, nymphs, etcetera. The guardian guides or benevolent spirits that help in the spiritual evolution and in some cases even angels and extraterrestrials.

For people who are skeptical, all this will seem unbelievable, but in fact there is a way to prove the existence of all the above written.

The astral plane is of a certain practicable access since it borders next to our 3D. For those who wish to know it, they should only study, (with great attention and accompanied by enlightened masters), a practice called "astral unfolding".

Here we also find the memory of the Matrix, known as the **"akashic records"**, a kind of energetic or quantum space, where the past, present and future of the Cosmos are stored.

To put it in our own words: it is a kind of virtual library that houses not only our thoughts, actions or experiences, but also those of all places and beings on the planet. All information is energetically recorded in a cosmic memory bank.

By accessing this memory we can navigate through the mind of the holographic and know the deep mysteries of the metaphysical spheres.

5) The fifth dimension: eternity.

It is a non-physical energetic frequency. Time is a circular continuum, there is only the eternal now.

Here the illusory world of matter disappears to conceive a vibrational frequency that is pure energy.

In this dimension is where an even greater expansion of consciousness is experienced. It is the connection with the Supraconsciousness that relates to the perception that all is one. It is a great shift in consciousness that has to do with understanding that we are part of the whole.

We connect with the Consciousness at a group level that forms a single being of greater dimensions. It is the dimension where we merge with the group to which we vibrationally belong and the higher or multidimensional being. In other words, within this world, the individual consciousness merges with the different groups of souls that have the same vibratory level, becoming one single spirit.

It is the dimension where we remember who we are and awaken our inner wise.

The fifth dimension is the frequency of wisdom, where we find the ascended masters and spirit guides, the beings of light that guide men in their spiritual development (those called Angels), free souls in an infinite Universe that goes beyond time and space, that is why it is called eternity.

From the fifth dimension on, the dimensions are fused and their boundaries are blurred or rather vanish.

This is because we are talking about pure energy and not matter.

6) The Sixth Dimension: The Sacred Matrix

The sixth dimension is called the Christic or Buddhic dimension, because it is here that one reaches the state of total remembrance; where one takes responsibility for the whole and is the whole. It is known by mystics as the true reality, which Buddhists call **"Nirvana"** and Christians call **"heaven"**. It is a state of compassionate awareness, the state of Enlightenment. It is the return Home, to the One Self.

In the sixth dimension, the process of evolution of the self and the whole are experienced as one.

It is the place of unlimited and unified consciousness. That consciousness manifests as individual and collective simultaneously. The sixth dimension is the creator of the morphogenic matrices that manifest in other dimensions as third, second and first. These matrices are the geometric forms and networks that we call sacred geometry. They are the geometric patterns of light, creators of life and responsible for its materialization. This is where thoughts materialize immediately. There is no evil here, so thoughts are always positive. Only positive energies materialize. Here lies the enlightened consciousness and the numerological matrix in the form of wisdom, as if it were a great library, which is located one step away from God.

7) The seventh dimension: the home of God.

It is the frequency of total integration. There are no more scattered parts. Here are the beings who are in the energy of love, and are pure love. It is an energetic dimension where the spiritual body overlaps the physical body. It is the dimension of pure light consciousness.

The divine source of all cosmic existence. Consciousness is experienced multidimensionally.

Although some claim that there are perhaps as many as 14 dimensions, it is known that there is a point of vibrational frequency above the consciousness in which the different worlds are no longer perceived as separate to be integrated with the one, or what the Hindus call: the brahman or atman and in the soul, mind and body of the cosmos, in the last state of consciousness, dwells the Supreme Spirit that created the absolute.

Those pure souls who have been able to contemplate the radiance of this inexplicable dimension affirm that it is the Abode of God.

The realities of other dimensions and other levels are not beyond the reach of the human being; on the contrary, they are within him, they are part of his life, for all that exists is Consciousness.

You could be living, right now and without realizing it, the experience of ascending to a higher level with respect to the 3rd dimension.

Learn how to recognize it with the following signs:

1_ it may seem that everything remains the same on an external level, **you feel that something inside you,** which you cannot explain well, **has changed,** because you no longer perceive things around you in the same way. You have **become an observer of everything, including yourself.** You feel that everything is seen more clearly, and you feel that you no longer occupy the same place as before. This can make you feel somewhat strange and at the same time serene.

2_ Instead of forcing reality to go your way, **you begin to accept life as it presents itself.**

In the 5th dimension, you are beginning to experience a moment of openness, expansion and acceptance. You understand that you must resonate with your inner self, therefore, you no longer worry about making the best decision and controlling everything. You prefer to leave it in the hands of your intuition. You feel that if you let yourself flow, life will put you in front of the path you should go through, without forcing situations.

3_ You become more spiritual. You have already left aside your ego that has made you live feelings of guilt, victimization, bad luck, karma. Now you begin to understand that everything has its meaning, that nothing happens by chance and that from every difficulty there is a learning experience waiting for you. Whether it is helping you heal, showing you something to learn, or simply pointing you in the right direction; each person or situation is unique and deserves your deeper attention from the physical plane.

4_ You will begin to perceive a more pleasant world and your high vibration will attract better situations and people that will open doors for you and you will feel more fulfilled, because **you will have freed yourself from the attachments of the physical world to see beyond, where everything becomes much more subtle.**

If you are experiencing a difficult situation, accept it and do not get discouraged. **As soon as the whole of humanity begins to awaken its consciousness in Love, we will be able to achieve the healing of souls.** Finally, we will understand that **everything we have lived through will have been a great learning of love, empathy and trust in the Universe.**

CHAPTER 3

THE UNIVERSE IS A HOLOGRAM

"The entire cosmos is wrapped up in every cell of our body", David Bohm.

...just like every tree leaf, every raindrop, and every fish in the ocean, giving a deep meaning to the famous poem by **William Blake**:

"To see a world in a grain of sand
And a sky in a wild flower,
To embrace infinity in the palm of one's hand
And eternity in an hour."

In a hologram, every part is within the whole, and the whole is within each part. However, what's most important is that **each part has access to the whole.**

If the brain were to function like a hologram, we might speculate that it would have access to a greater whole, a sphere of holistic frequency that transcends the boundaries of space and time.

Based on discoveries in quantum mechanics, several physicists have postulated the idea that the third dimension is a holographic Universe.

I'm particularly interested in the reasoning proposed by scientist **David Bohm. Thanks to his explanation of the "implicate" and "explicate" orders, we can gain a better understanding of the difference in meaning between two terms in the Spanish language: CONSCIENCIA (UNIVERSAL CONSCIOUSNESS) and CONCIENCIA (INDIVIDUAL CONSCIENCE),** which can often be confused.

David Bohm became convinced that the Universe itself was a kind of giant, fluid hologram. He published his initial work in the early 1970s, and in 1980, he compiled his thoughts into a book titled "Wholeness and the Implicate Order." In it, he asserts that the tangible reality of our daily lives is, in fact, a kind of illusion, much like a holographic image.

This introduces a new way of looking at reality, which is as incredible as it is radical. **Bohm** talks about "enfolded orders and unfolded realities."

When we analyze the holographic image that we perceive with our human sensory senses, we need to understand that this projection of reality stems from a deeper order of existence, a level of reality that is infinitely vast and primary, giving rise to all the objects and appearances in the physical world, much like a holographic plate or matrix gives rise to the hologram. **Bohm** refers to this deeper level of reality as the "implicate" or "enfolded" order. Then, he designates our three-dimensional level of existence as the "explicate" or "unfolded" order.

This "implicate" order, which is indivisible and envelops everything while giving rise to all things that exist, is "UNIVERSAL CONSCIOUSNESS." On the other hand, the "explicate" or "unfolded" order, perceived through our senses, this projection of the observer or one's own description of reality, this sensory and moral framework for distinguishing what is right from what is wrong based on our personal beliefs, and how each of us projects and sees the material world we live **in, is "INDIVIDUAL CONSCIENCE.**

In other words, **the INDIVIDUAL CONSCIENCE (CONCIENCIA) is ENVELOPED by the UNIVERSAL CONSCIOUSNESS (CONSCIENCIA) of the Whole.**

David Bohm speaks of **enfolded orders and unfolded realities** because he sees the manifestation of all forms in the Universe as the result of countless involvements and unfoldments between these two orders.

Information is distributed non-locally, and both orders contain a myriad of possibilities.

Bohm prefers to describe the Universe using the term **"holomovement"** because it conveys the dynamic and ever-active nature of the countless involvements and unfoldments that create the Universe moment by moment. While the term **"hologram"** often refers to a relatively static image, which, according to him, doesn't quite do justice to it. For example, when electrons move, they take on the same shape that a geyser assumes when it bursts forth from a mountain. They are sustained by a constant inflow from the implicate order.

An electron isn't a thing but rather the totality or entirety enfolded throughout all of space. The hologram projected from the film represents the explicate order because it depicts the perceptible and unfolded version of the image. The continuous and fluid interplay between the two orders explains how particles can change shape and transform from one type of particle to another. It also clarifies that a quantum can manifest as a particle or a wave based on how the observer interacts with the whole. **Bohm** rejects the idea that particles don't exist until they are observed. As all these aspects are facets of the holomovement, **Bohm** believes that it doesn't make sense to talk about interaction between consciousness and matter. The quantum or holistic observer knows that they are intervening in what they are observing and that they are also changing or affecting their surroundings.

What is the Observer in Quantum Physics?

Quantum theory holds that the observer of an event influences the way that event is perceived. It's similar to saying that the same tennis ball may appear as a sphere to one person and a cube to another.

The role of the observer in determining the form a quantum takes isn't any more mysterious than that of a jeweler when handling a precious stone and deciding which facets will be visible and which won't.

In fact, consciousness is a subtle form of matter and the basis for all interactions between the two. This relationship doesn't exist at the level of our reality but rather in the depths of the implicate order. Consciousness is present to varying degrees in the enfoldment and unfoldment of matter, and that might be why plasmas possess characteristics of living things. "Even a rock, in a way, is alive", **Bohm** asserts, because life and intelligence are not only present in all matter but also in "energy," "space," "time," and "the fabric of the entire Universe."

Bohm tells us: "Take a moment to think about this. Look at your hand. Now look at the light emanating from the lamp next to you. Look at the cat resting at your feet. It's not just that you are made of the same stuff. You are the same thing. One thing. Undivided. An immense something that has stretched its countless arms and appendages out to all visible objects, to atoms, turbulent seas, and the twinkling stars of the cosmos."

The Universe is the undivided totality of all things. **Bohm** cautions that this doesn't mean the Universe is a giant undifferentiated mass. Things can be part of an undivided whole and possess unique qualities of their own, like the little whirlpools that often form in rivers. It's impossible to determine where one whirlpool ends and the river begins. **Bohm** isn't implying that differences between "things" lack meaning; he simply wants us to know that the theoretical division into "things" depends on our perception and thought processes. Instead of "things," he prefers to call them relatively autonomous sub-totalities of the holomovement.

In conclusion, **Bohm** believes that the nearly universal tendency to fragment the world and ignore the dynamic interconnection that exists among all things is the cause of many problems, not only in the field of science but also in our lives and society.

For instance, we believe we can extract valuable parts from the Earth without affecting the whole. We think it's possible to treat individual parts of the body without concerning ourselves with the entirety. We believe we can address various societal issues like crime, poverty, or drug addiction without studying these issues as part of the whole of society.

Therefore, the current way of fragmenting the world into parts not only doesn't work but can potentially lead us to extinction.

Is the Universe an Illusion?

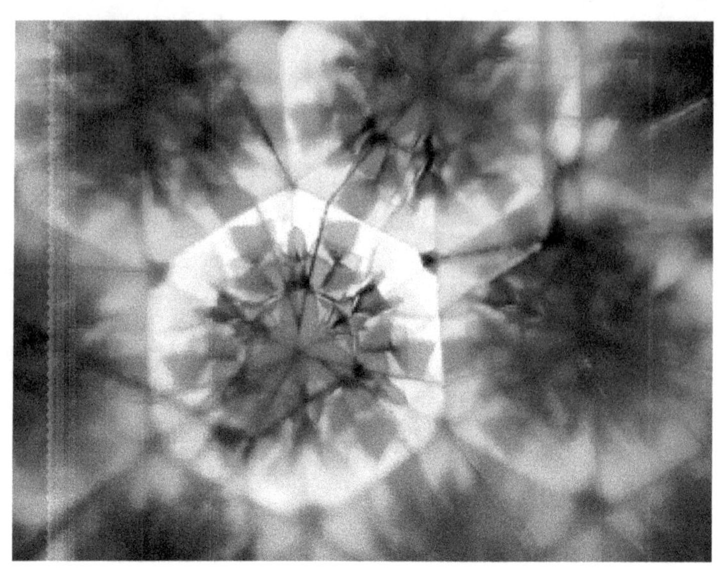

When I was a little girl, I was gifted a **kaleidoscope**. I loved spending hours playing and creating a thousand and one combinations of colorful and sensational images, imagining new fantastic worlds in my dreamy mind.

kaleidoscope (from the Greek words kalós, meaning beautiful, éidos, meaning image, and scopéo, meaning to observe) is a tube that contains three mirrors, forming a triangular prism with its reflective side inward. At the end of these mirrors, there are two translucent sheets with various objects of different colors and shapes between them. When you turn the tube while looking through the opposite end, the images of these objects are symmetrically multiplied. The mirrors can be arranged at different angles.

Like the game of the kaleidoscope, the hologram is an optical illusion because it displays something different from reality.

In physics terms, the intersection of lights reflecting the hologram is processed in the brain as a three-dimensional object based on the information received by the eyes. Therefore, the illusion is an erroneous or partial perception of reality.

Our brain is a computer that processes information. In a modern life filled with stimuli, we are bombarded with vast amounts of information every second. However, the brain only processes a tiny fraction of it. Out of the 400 billion bits of information per second, scientific studies have shown that we are only consciously aware of about 2,000 bits related to the environment, time, and our bodies. Hence, **what we consider reality, what we experience, is just a small part of what is actually happening.**

Human beings perceive their environment through their senses, which send information to the human brain for interpretation. Many times, this information undergoes distortion caused by the senses' misinterpretation or deception. Our beliefs also play a role; the model of what we believe about the world is constructed from our inner feelings and ideas. This suggests that humans possess immense mental potential beyond what is commonly believed. This is evident in conditions referred to as paranormal.

The holographic paradigm was born from this concept, an attempt to demonstrate that **the brain is a hologram perceiving and participating in a holographic Universe.** Therefore, we can assume that we do not live in objective worlds but that **our worlds are a reflection of our entirely subjective interpretation.** We are not aware that everything we observe, think, feel, say, or do passes through a filter, which is our own system of beliefs, paradigms, prejudices, and the personal way we perceive reality. The world we see and perceive may be nothing more than an illusion partially created by our minds.

Each piece of information we receive from the outside world is processed based on our past experiences, and our emotional response is derived from these memories. This is why bad memories often lead us to repeat the same mistakes. How we interpret the world, whether positively or negatively, also depends on our emotional state, our attitude, and how we react to any situation. That's why everything is relative. For example, someone who promotes war creates an egotistical vision of their world based on power, dominance, wealth, and destruction to achieve their own ends. On the other hand, a person who has a vision connected to the Supraconscious mind based on the feeling of pure love will build their world in harmony with creation and cooperation.

In Eastern philosophy, the Universe is considered an **illusion, Maya**, or, as **Calderón De la Barca** put it, a **dream.** What each person creates in their world is a product of their own consciousness. **Depending on whether it is imbued with positive Supraconsciousness or negative egomania, it will shape their own illusory reality with certain characteristics.**

For some mystics, this illusory manifestation of appearances is real because they are immersed in it.

Every person or physical object, from the perspective of eternity, is like a brief and disturbed drop of water in an endless ocean.

A Reflection of the Universe and Our Blue Planet by Carl Sagan

It is well known to scientists and philosophers of classical antiquity that the Earth is an insignificant point in the vast cosmos. But no one had ever seen it like this; (Photo taken from Saturn by the Voyager probe in 1990.)

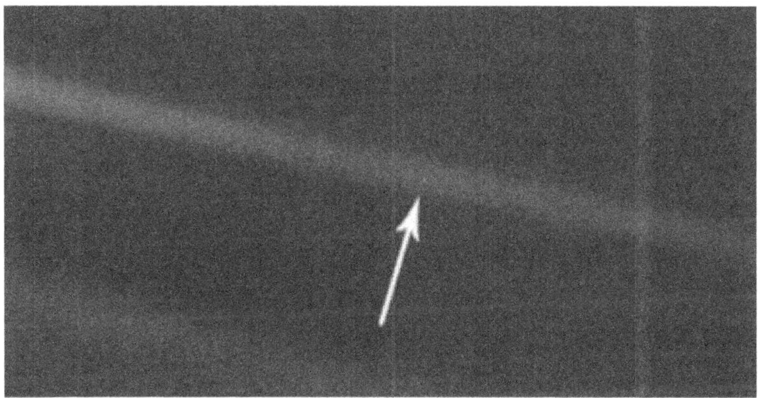

The astronomer **Carl Sagan** wrote a book entitled **"A Pale Blue Dot"**, in which he captures a set of reflections about the possibilities of the human race in the Universe.

In an excerpt from the First Chapter of this book he says:

"In this image there is no sign of human beings, nothing of our work on the surface, neither of our machines, nor of ourselves. From this point of view, there is no evidence of our nationalist obsession; on the scale of the worlds, human beings are insignificant, a thin layer of life on a dark and lonely piece of rock and metal.

Consider again at that dot. That's here. That's home. That's us. On it everyone you love, everyone you know, everyone you ever heard of, every human being who ever was, lived out their lives. The aggregate of our joy and suffering, thousands of confident religions, ideologies, and economic doctrines, every hunter and forager, every hero and coward, every creator

and destroyer of civilization, every king and peasant, every young couple in love, every mother and father, hopeful child, inventor and explorer, every teacher of morals, every corrupt politician, every "superstar," every "supreme leader," every saint and sinner in the history of our species lived there—on a mote of dust suspended in a sunbeam.

The Earth is a very small stage in a vast cosmic arena. Think of the rivers of blood spilled by all those generals and emperors so that, in glory and triumph, they could become the momentary masters of a fraction of a dot. Think of the endless cruelties visited by the inhabitants of one corner of this pixel on the scarcely distinguishable inhabitants of some other corner, how frequent their misunderstandings, how eager they are to kill one another, how fervent their hatreds.

Our posturings, our imagined self-importance, the delusion that we have some privileged position in the Universe, are challenged by this point of pale light. Our planet is a lonely speck in the great enveloping cosmic dark. In our obscurity, in all this vastness, there is no hint that help will come from elsewhere to save us from ourselves.

The Earth is the only world known so far to harbor life. There is nowhere else, at least in the near future, to which our species could migrate. Visit, yes. Settle, not yet. Like it or not, for the moment the Earth is where we make our stand.

It has been said that astronomy is a humbling and character-building experience. There is perhaps no better demonstration of the folly of human conceits than this distant image of our tiny world. To me, it underscores our responsibility to deal more kindly with one another, and to preserve and cherish the pale blue dot, the only home we've ever known."

CHAPTER 4

THE 12 UNIVERSAL LAWS
THE MEANING OF LIFE

What have we come to do in this world?

Connecting with our Higher Self or Supraconsciousness leads us to open up to **awakening and receive the Being that exists within us**; to feel who we are, what we are, how we are; to know why and for what purpose we are what we are... **Our Higher Self** knows that we have a purpose that goes far beyond our ego and our fears.

We've come to this world to learn, to evolve, and to be happy.

The general message we receive from all spiritual teachers is reflected in this concept: There's not a single moment in your life when you don't have everything you need to be happy. The reason you're unhappy is that you keep thinking about what you don't have, instead of thinking, rather, about what you have right now.

We must learn to find happiness in the smallest things in life, in the simple pleasures it gives us every day.

The problem is that most people equate happiness with obtaining what they're attached to, and they don't want to admit that happiness lies precisely in their absence, and in not being subject to the power of any person or thing... because happiness resides within ourselves!

Certainly... we haven't come to merely survive! If you don't know what you've come to do in this world, you have to discover it to give your life meaning. Living without a purpose won't do you any good because others will lead you to do all sorts of things. When you have a **very clear goal**, when you know where you're headed, the Universe opens up paths for you.

King Solomon said, "A people without a vision perish, die."

Socrates said, "There is no wind that can favor a ship that doesn't know where it's going"...

Plato said, "Everything we are depends on the world of ideas"...

Buddha said, "We are what we think"...

Therefore, if we don't find meaning in our lives... we're going to be inside a bottle floating in the middle of the ocean, drifting aimlessly!

Do you remember in my first book of the saga **LEARNING: ABSOLUTE POWER**, I told you about the **POWER OF QUESTIONS**? Well, you need to ask yourself questions because that's where you'll find the answers. The answer you seek is in the questions we ask ourselves as we journey through this thing called life.

What is it that you truly love to do in this life?

What do you want from life?

What are you good at that sets you apart and helps others evolve with you?

When you have a purpose, you need to put it into action without wasting time. The Universe is your friend. The Universe is a mental game. The Universe is a game of attention because it is Pure Creative Energy.

"Where your attention goes, your energy goes, and that's what you become," said **Conde Saint Germain.**

Understanding the laws that govern the Universe can help us find the answers to these existential questions and give meaning to our lives, starting to perceive reality differently and reacting with a different attitude to the challenges we overcome along the way.

1_ The Law of UNITY
We are all One!

There's a **Golden Rule** that **Jesus of Nazareth** made quite clear, which says, **"Treat others as you would like to be treated."**

When we manage to awaken our dormant consciousness and enter that spiritual dimension of harmony, peace, and joy; when we finally connect with our **Inner Self, our Higher Self**, in other words, **Supraconsciousness, we then experience a sense of openness and become part of the WHOLE. We feel that we are all connected...** When we look at the image of a rose, **we now see its essence.**

Likewise, we see other people as ourselves because they are our siblings. That's why everything you do to others, you are doing to yourself because we are all one, and we are all interconnected with that Non-Local Consciousness, which is the First Intelligence that created us and is within us.

2_ The Law of VIBRATION

The entire Universe is vibrating because everything is energy.

Every human mind or brain is both a broadcasting and receiving station for the frequency vibrations of our thoughts... These electromagnetic waves are already vibrating in the Universe and, like a spider's web, they will attract to you, through the law of attraction, everything that vibrates at your same frequency. That's why we say: **THINK POSITIVE.**

Mental conditioning emits a vibration that always attracts situations, people, and events that vibrate on the same wave frequency. Therefore, in the realm of money, for example... if you are neurologically conditioned not to have money because your beliefs are rooted in poverty, and poverty is your comfort zone that your mind tries to protect, anything that deviates from that, your mind rejects. It's a game of the subconscious that can't be avoided. On the other hand, the very need to obtain more wealth will create more poverty because it makes you vibrate in scarcity, attracting more of the same and causing all the abundance and money that were available to you to flow to other places with the same vibration. The solution is to remain calm during the creative process and reprogram your mind to vibrate in abundance, appreciating every little thing you already have. Because... if you can't appreciate what you have, you'll never be able to appreciate what the Universe has in store for you. It's a process of reconditioning your neurons to attract money. The premise is to conceive any change in your life as a positive thing and vibrate at a high frequency; otherwise, you will revert to the negative low-frequency vibration of scarcity.

The danger may be real, but FEAR is a choice that a person chooses to live with because... FEAR doesn't exist.

The world we live in is a world with its dangers and its stories, but ATTENTION!

It's important to know that if you do things with fear, you are sending that message to the quantum field, and unintentionally creating a reality where you will experience the same fear you are trying to reject.

There are people **who live in fear**, without even knowing what they are afraid of or why! These are individuals who live disconnected, in the **false belief that they are alone, abandoned,** and **separated from Everything**, which is **Divine Creation and is us.**

Let's remember that since we are all interconnected, all we have to do is flow and let things come as they may because there's a Perfect Order in the Universe.

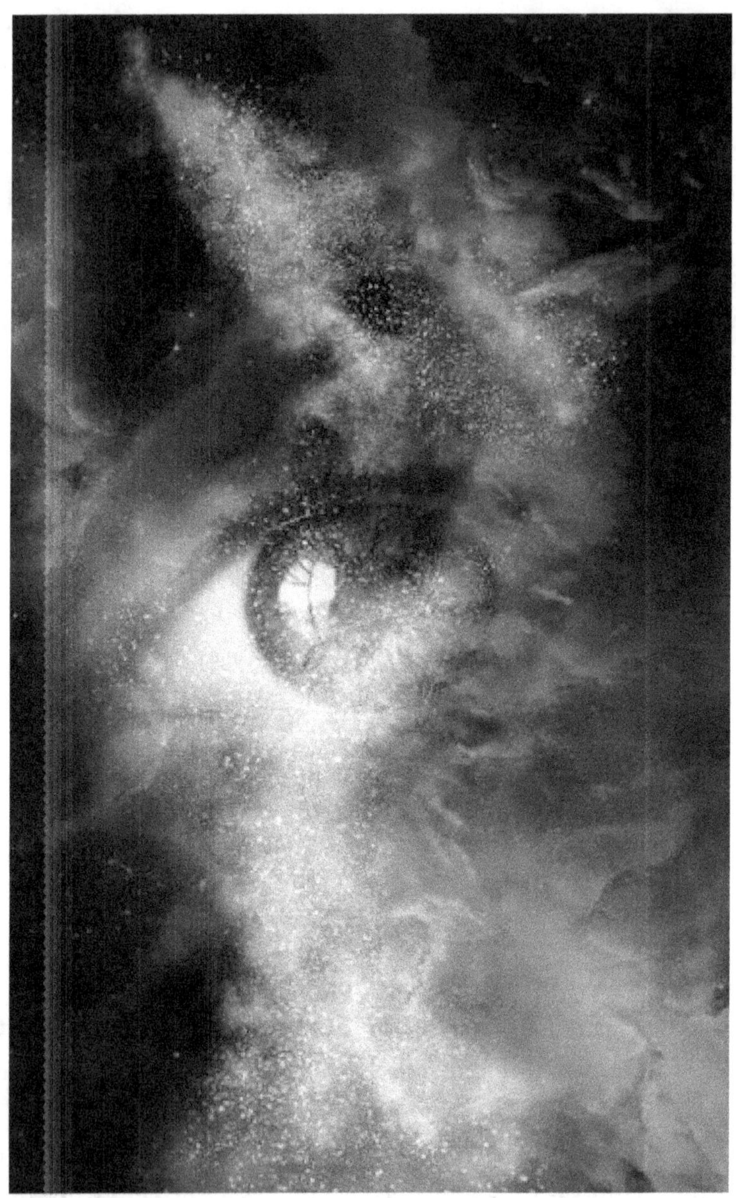

If you live an experience that bothers you, don't think it's just bad luck. Think that this is what's meant to be, maybe to prevent worse things from happening. Everything is perfect; that's becoming aware.

What situations still cause you some suffering or fear? Remember this piece of wisdom that says:

"What you fear most will come upon you"... Or another one that says: "If you don't like the broth, you'll get two servings."

What do these two phrases mean?

It means that what I don't like is precisely what I need to accept and embrace. The more I resist it, the stronger life presents it to me due to the law of vibration. So, if I resist the broth, it multiplies, two, three, four, or even five servings... But if I stop resisting it, it won't manifest at all. It's the same with fear.

What I'm afraid of is what I resist, and by resisting it, it manifests.

Everything you resist persists!

If I accept it, it doesn't need to manifest anymore.

3_ The Law of ACTION

To identify a person's level of consciousness, you need to know where they focus their attention. Stop looking around, at problems, other people's lives, and concentrate on the present because that's how you create a promising future.

If you believe it, you can create it.

You can be, do, or have anything you believe in. But since nothing comes for free, to get what you want, you have to take action. The key is to act. So, get out there to pursue your dreams, doing everything within your reach and doing it the best you can.

Jesus of Nazareth said, "Practice makes perfect."

Open yourself up to receive the vital force of the Universe that motivates you to move.

Taking action is what connects you with your Spiritual Self.

The moment you have a desire, it's an indicator that you have the power inside you to act on it, to bring it into reality with your talents. That power is God, and action is the bridge connecting the metaphysical or quantum world with the physical or material world.

You need to take action to get a reaction: if you sow good seeds, you'll have a good plant; if you sow bad seeds, you'll have a bad plant, but if you don't sow anything, you'll still get weeds... You have to take action to be extraordinary; that extra effort, that 1% that no one wants to make, that extra mile that others don't want to go, is what will set you apart from everyone else, and by doing that, you'll achieve different results, which some call success, and others call luck... But we all know that luck doesn't exist! You create your own luck by deciding at each step the actions you'll take... You're creating your world moment by moment with your decisions and actions.

"Success is just one decision away"[12], **Jack Baker** reminds us in his saga of **"The Initiates"** .

Not taking risks won't make you lose, but it won't make you win either. "No calm sea has ever made a skilled sailor." Good sailors train in stormy seas... leaving comfort behind to face the unknown is undoubtedly a vital incentive since the comfort zone doesn't allow us to grow. To evolve in life, you have to lean forward and take action, to take that first step without fear.

"The only universal antidote against fear is action, and therefore, every time I'm afraid, I know I have to act. [...] Seeking action is what can get me out of fear" [...] "Fears and worries can steal our happiness; we must learn to live without fears" [...] "Whatever needs to happen will happen, living in fear only deprives us of our happiness," says **Jorge Bucay.**

4_The Law of CORRESPONDENCE

Hermes Trismegistus, in the Kybalion, said: "As above, so below, as within, so without."

According to the law of correspondence, all human beings, without exception, are located in the perfect place to acquire the exact learning they came into the physical world for. The law of correspondence creates the perfect circumstances for everything to manifest and occur in each place, in such a way that nobody experiences anything they aren't supposed to.

Therefore, it's futile to go against the law. No matter how much we want, strive, and fight for it, we can't change what we're meant to live. The best attitude in this case is to either stop fighting or accept the law, to put ourselves back into the Universe's order.

If, on the other hand, we insist on something that isn't meant for us, like a job or a relationship, we act against the law of correspondence, which is not only useless but generates all sorts of blockages: if it's meant to be, things flow; if it's not meant to be, everything is blocked.

Everyone should do the best they know how, but anything that isn't in their power isn't meant to be. If it can be done, it's because it's meant to be, and it will be perfect. But when we start suffering over things we can't change, we're fighting against life.

To change the correspondences, I need to change my way of thinking, feeling, and seeing life. Thus, I change my correspondences, but I don't change the Universe. This is the essential understanding in Aceptology: we're not going to change the Universe because reality isn't changeable. What's changeable is the individual experience. What changes is my experience. The environment's experience doesn't change; the person who alters the environment against the will of others is the one who will suffer. What I can do is change roles, activities, places, and change personal experiences. The Law of Correspondence dictates the specific life experiences a person undergoes, where and when they occur, and how they relate to one's evolutionary needs. It also defines the roles an individual must assume in their chosen place and outlines their mission of love and service, along with the recipients of this service. In all situations, there's a dual purpose: learning and teaching.

Long before birth, every person's gender, race, parents, nationality, role, and all associated experiences have been predetermined based on the infinite plan and mission corresponding exactly to their level of consciousness in that body to continue their evolution process.

This is how the law of correspondence works: you get what you need to learn from each circumstance. Recognizing this allows us to understand that everyone lives a different but necessary and corresponding experience.

That's how the law of correspondence operates: it doesn't bring about what we want but what we need.

For our process of consciousness evolution, all we need to ask ourselves in any circumstance is: "What do I need to learn from this? Why am I experiencing this?" Because every situation we face is corresponding and exact for each one of us.

Recognizing this helps us understand that each person lives a different yet necessary and corresponding experience. Our problems are the result of our choices, but they don't make us guilty; they merely correspond to the outcome. It's not a punishment; it's a result. When we learn to see the value in every experience and enjoy what we often call difficulties, nothing becomes a problem but rather a tool for work and an opportunity for learning. Therefore, challenging situations aren't unfair.

There is no unfair situation; everything that has happened, is happening now, and will happen in our lives is the result of our own correspondences. We have no reason to blame anything or anyone for what we go through.

5_ The law of CAUSE AND EFFECT

In the Bible, **Jesus of Nazareth** tells us that: "**What you sow, you reap**".

Thoughts are the cause that brings about the effects in your life. Therefore if you change your thoughts, you will change the results in your life.

However, a problem is that 90% of people create their reality through unconscious thoughts that are already programmed by belief systems. These beliefs determine their vibration and attract circumstances, people, and opportunities that vibrate at the same frequencies they emit, even if they're unaware of it. So, it's clear that luck, as traditionally perceived, doesn't exist.

"Until the unconscious becomes conscious, the subconscious will direct your life, and you will call it destiny."

Carl Gustav Jung

Don't become a slave to your unconscious mind, which seeks to control everything. When you take charge of your life and become aware of your inner truth, you'll experience true freedom.

If you genuinely want to achieve the results you've set for yourself in material aspects of life, whether in the realm of money, health, or love, you must work on your Inner Self, the cause that reflects outward and produces the effects or results you desire.

Reality is created by an intelligent entity that collapses energy into matter. Therefore, we are creators through the attention we give to things, which later materializes in the physical realm.

Using the analogy of a two-sided mirror, real image represents our Spiritual Self, and the reflection of that image on the physical side is what we believe ourselves to be in appearance.

Applying the formula of creation, where thoughts lead to emotions, emotions lead to actions, and actions lead to results, we see that there are no futile thoughts. Every thought produces an effect on some level. So, be vigilant about your thoughts, as everything has a cause and effect. This is a universal law.

Remember, if you harm others, harm will come back to you; if you act with goodness, goodness will return to you. This is the Golden Rule. Changing something you dislike in the external world requires altering the causes that generate the effects. It's crucial to look inward to change your beliefs, paradigms, thoughts, and emotions that lead to your actions in order to change your results.

The world is a reflection of our lives and beliefs. If you want to live in peace, you have to find peace within yourself first, and then it will manifest in the external world, despite the chaos that surrounds us.

6_ The Law of COMPENSATION

Jesus of Nazareth reminds us in **A Course in Miracles: "To have, you have to give everything to everyone."**

Related to the preceding law, if you've done well with the law of cause and effect, the Universe will compensate you with this law of giving and receiving.

Jesus of Nazareth explained it with the parable of the harvest: "What you've sown, you shall reap."

The entire Universe comes through channels of love, business, and health. It depends on what you dedicate to each of these channels, that's what the Universe will compensate you with. Fear is nothing, and love is everything. You choose: one or the other.

7_ The Law of ATTRACTION

We attract everything that vibrates on our frequency. It's a variation of the principle of vibration that says, **"Everything vibrating at our frequency is drawn to us. Similar vibrations resonate together, while those that don't separate."**

You don't attract what you want; you attract what you believe.

You don't attract what you desire; you attract what you are.

People also form communities based on their likes, interests, ways of thinking, and feeling. We relate through resonances and polarities. Your perception merely reflects your mental state. The world's stage is the best way for me to understand what my beliefs are and what I'm attracting into my life. We attract complementary polarities, those with whom we resonate. If we want to know what we're projecting, we have to observe what we're receiving.

8_ The Law of TRANSMUTATION

The mind is the screen on which the heart projects: if the heart is turbid, thoughts will be too; if the heart is accelerated, thoughts will be too. Just as the principle of rhythm says that everything changes, your energy can also change with the power of your thoughts. We know that as co-creators with the Universe through our Primary Intelligence, we can collapse energy and transform it into matter. In other words, if you're vibrating at a negative or harmful energy, you can transmute the situation yourself by raising your energy to a higher vibration and, from the heart, with the power of your positive thoughts, you can find the solution to your problems among the infinite possibilities available to us.

You are the Alchemist or Creator God of your own life!

Remember that if there's a problem, the problem is in your mind. To solve a problem, you first need to resolve your thoughts, and as a consequence, everything else gets fixed.

As long as you limit yourself to recognizing only the need for the remedy, you'll continue to have fear, and fear will paralyze you. However, as soon as you accept that the remedy is within you, you'll have discarded fear and will begin to act.

The remedy is in the source...
This is how true healing takes place.
Don't heal the fish; heal the water!
Victor Frankl reflects:
"When the situation is good, enjoy it;
When the situation is bad, transform it;
When the situation cannot be transformed,
then transform yourself.
But never try to change anyone.
In any case, change yourself first."
9_ The Law of RELATIVITY
Your life depends on your attitude in the face of the situations presented to you.

"The last of the human freedoms: to choose one's attitude in any given set of circumstances, to choose one's own way. And there were always choices to make. Every day, every hour, offered the opportunity to make a decision, a decision which determined whether you would or would not submit to those powers which threatened to rob you of your very self, your inner freedom; which determined whether or not you become the plaything to circumstance, renouncing freedom and dignity..."
Victor Frankl, Man's Search For Ultimate Meaning.

Frankl understood this reality firsthand. When he was sent to the Nazi death camps, he could not alter his situation. However, he tried his best to give his suffering meaning by changing his attitude toward it. He thought about re-uniting with his wife or finishing his manuscript, should he ever be freed. This gave him drive.

Everything in life is relative and depends on our reactions to what happens to us. The Universe conspires for our good and favor. Everything comes into our life for us to learn the lesson and continue evolving. The Universe has two poles: positive and negative. Pleasure protects us, and we accept it; pain threatens us, and we reject it. So, our beliefs' values are twofold: good or bad. But since everything is relative, it all depends on how we react in each situation.

10_ The law of POLARITY

We're not very aware that we live in a polarized world. In reality, **the two poles don't oppose each other but complement each other and are as necessary and vital for our existence.** The positive complements the negative, the masculine complements the feminine, and this polarity keeps us intrinsically united. If we were to try to eliminate a polarity, we would actually cease to exist. Therefore, this **dual world, this polarized world that seems to be separate, is, in reality, united because we are all interconnected. So, polarities are two sides of the same coin.**

In the Bible, **Saint Paul** said in Romans 12:2 that: "**We are transformed by the renewal of our minds**". Therefore, we don't have to settle for this world's model; instead, we should take control of our lives and become new and better people. We're going to empty the past and fill it with the new, replace the bad with the good, and transform the negative into positive.

The wisdom of living and growing between polarities is to have what is called a paradoxical mindset. It's the ability to understand that everything has its opposites, which, in the end, are complementary. Accepting their demands and assuming that what opposes you actually strengthens you activates your mind and creativity to find solutions beyond what you thought existed. The conflict between opposites is the basis of all existence.

Lao Tzu said regarding the TAO that IT IS AND IT ISN'T.

In the same way, we reconnect with quantum physics for which light is both wave and particle, meaning it is a potentiality.

We are APPEARANCE and we are ESSENCE...

In the Bible, in the Gospel of Matthew, we are told that: "WHAT IS, ISN'T. WHAT ISN'T, IS."

WHAT IS, IS: what we see in appearance, matter, the body, the ego, even if we believe it is, it ISN'T because it is incredibly ephemeral, transient, and temporary.

WHAT ISN'T, IS: what we can't see with the naked eye is the essence, the soul, the eternal, which exists in each of us, human beings, and which we feel but can't see. **It's the spirit, the energy, the intuition, the cause of all that is created.**

Therefore, with the concept of paradox and its integration, the mind reaches another level of consciousness. When we confront the paradox, integrating its opposites, we shatter preconceived ideas. Accepting that both opposites always reveals the truth, once the opposites are unified and merged, the deep cosmic and hidden unity of things is revealed.

The truth is the perfection we find in the Supraconscious mind, which is the First Cause, which is ourselves.

So, how do you change and overcome difficulties?

First, you must become aware of your emotional state in a particular critical situation by asking yourself the following question:

Where are you focusing your attention?

On the problem or the solution?

Which side are you on?

You are as big as the difficulties you overcome.

You are as small as the obstacle that stops you.

If you want to change any negative situation, just shift your attention to the opposite pole through your thoughts and set aside your fears. If you want to move from poverty to wealth, from illness to health, from lovelessness to love, you must repolarize the negative into positive.

Don't ask for water while crossing the desert; ask for wisdom!

11_ The Law of RHYTHM

Everything is in motion; everything is changing. You must adapt to all situations through action.

Heraclitus of Ephesus said: "EVERYTHING FLOWS." EVERY-THING CHANGES, EVERYTHING MOVES, NOTHING REMAINS. We are never the same. "No one bathes in the same river twice" because neither the person nor the river is the same a moment later.

A river has moving water, so when we go out and get back in, we don't get wet with the same water; in other words, it's not exactly the same river.

You must direct your actions for your own good. If you work on your body, you will have health. If you do nothing, you'll end up sick, aging, and weak. If you don't contribute to your relationship, you'll end up in lovelessness. If you don't work on what you love, you'll end up poor, doing what others tell you to do. So, you have to take control of your life, and your results will depend on how you manage that change.

Where there's life, there's change. And if there's change, adaptations must necessarily happen.

Lao Tse gave us this wonderful reflection about it:

"In life, man is elastic and evolves. At the moment of death, he is rigid and unchangeable. Plants in the sun are flexible and fibrous, but they perish dry and cracked. Therefore, what is elastic and flexible is associated with life, and what is rigid and unchangeable is associated with death."

More than standing firm like steel, life demands that we flow like water.

"Be like water, my friend, be like water that flows and never stagnates, keep flowing," said Bruce Lee.

Few elements are as inspiring and conducive to change as water. One of the **three qualities of water,** according to Taoism, as extracted from the poetry of **Lao Tzu,** is **change**—an option to be made without fear. When the temperature is extreme, water can become ice or vapor. It can change its form depending on where it is. It becomes a glass when contained, insignificant when trapped in a rock's crevice, regains its vastness when it returns to the ocean, and transforms into nourishment when a living being is thirsty and in need.

Water has power and character. It knows and understands that nothing is as important as proceeding with change when necessary. The environment and nature are often hostile, and those who do not adapt do not survive.

Another quality of water is **humility**: "The water that flows through a calm, placid, and harmonious river nourishes nature." When its level is normal, it reaches the banks, feeds the animals, and fosters the ideal balance for everything to work. But when the river becomes arrogant and carries a greater volume, everything changes. The force of its current wreaks havoc, destroying environments and affecting all living beings.

We should integrate this quality of water characterized by **tranquility** and **humility** because someone who is aware of who they truly are and doesn't pretend to be something they're not will always prefer calm over violence. And although they may occasionally resort to it due to external causes, like water, they eventually return to their course.

Moreover, they will choose serenity at all times to promote natural balance.

Water also has the quality of being ever **alert to opportunity:** in any difficulty, there is always a spot where the light of opportunity shines. No matter how turbulent our surroundings may be, no matter the obstacles, changes, intimidations, or sudden hurdles that appear in our path, we should be like water and apply that relentless force to regain our freedom. We should find that crack, that weakness in our opponent or obstacle, where a new path opens, a new opportunity to conquer it.

Let's not forget that, in a way, **water is a great opportunist**. It never hesitates to change shape, setting, or position to keep moving forward. Just as times change, if we want to evolve, we need to adapt. That's why, even though crises can be annoying, they are always marvelous opportunities that push us to change and evolve. On the contrary, if we try to control everything, seek solutions in past experiences, and attempt to predict an uncertain future, we will make the same mistakes over and over again.

12_ The Law of GENDER

Everything has a masculine and a feminine principle. **Jesus of Nazareth** said, **"When you unite the two, you will move mountains."** The masculine energy is the objective and current intention. On all levels, the feminine energy is creation and nurturing; it is love. To bring forth life, we need both masculine and feminine energies. To generate abundance in business, we also need masculine energy of purpose and objectivity, and feminine energy, which is control and care. In general, action is masculine energy, and creation is feminine energy. Just as in nature, everything has a gestation period, all our dreams need time to mature before they can be harvested.

The problem arises when you accelerate the natural pace of gestation, creating an imbalance that will disrupt the universal law of balance upon which everything in nature is based.

On an energetic level, the law of balance acts like a pendulum. Balance occurs when everything is stable. When it becomes unbalanced, it swings from one extreme to another due to an excess of inner intention. Therefore, if you have a life goal but attach too much importance to it, you'll get the opposite result. By being overly attached to your desire, you'll hit the pendulum hard, which will take you to the opposite extreme, meaning you'll get the exact opposite of what you desire, distancing you further from your goal and leading to complete frustration.

For example, in the realm of money, if you desperately need it and chase it with too much attachment, you'll generate excessive potential, activating counterbalancing forces with a decisive outcome, always in the opposite direction of your desires, distancing you further from your goal and ending in total frustration.

Reflection

The School of Life, according to the teachings of **Gerardo Schmedling**, consistently presents us with four fundamental problems:

1_ Problems of relationships.

2_ Economic problems (either scarcity or resources).

3_ Health problems.

4_ Location problems (the inability to adapt to a particular place). If a person doesn't feel comfortable at home, at work, in their country, or on the planet, then where can they go?

Every one of us, without exception, has had to face one of these problems or obstacles in our life at some point, whether sooner or later. If you find yourself in a situation of distress, fear, suffering, or stress, it means there's something you haven't been able to accept.

So we ask ourselves, how do I free myself from this situation? The answer is quite simple: by accepting it.

How do you accept it? By understanding it. And how do you understand it? By studying the laws that govern the Universe.

Starting with the concept that the universal field is an echo of our thoughts and, by the law of vibration, it returns everything that resonates on the same frequency we're emitting.

If something about the situation bothers me, I need to change it within myself, not externally, because it's my own mind that projected it.

Indeed, each person generates their own correspondence within the Universe.

The Plan for Life Renewal has 4 steps:

1_ OBSERVE what I'm suffering from.

2_ UNDERSTAND what I'm not accepting.

3_ Once identified, seek information to understand why these situations I don't accept occur. If I manage to understand why they happen and see their value and purpose, I **ACCEPT** them.

4_ By accepting them, my suffering disappears completely, and I enter into a new life experience, meaning I **LEARN**.

Life renewal manifests when:

I understand that gaining or losing a year means nothing in a human being's life. Each human being has their own learning pace, living an experience that is valuable to them. I don't have to blame anyone for the decisions I make. Thus, I accept that there is a valuable experience for me to make better decisions next time. That's when a person accepts and suffering ends.

Aceptology is a science.

By understanding, we have the tool to accept the order of the Universe. If we accept it, our suffering will disappear. When our suffering disappears, we start to love.

And if we begin to love, we start to flow with the perfect order of the Universe and fill ourselves with inner peace. This is how we transcend. Accepting reality (what happens in a place where I can act) means I will stop suffering about things I can't change, things that I shouldn't change, and things that don't need to change because the only thing that needs to change is inside of us. There's nothing outside that needs to change. Everything that happens outside, even if it's challenging for our minds to accept, is necessarily perfect for the Universe's process. That's the general idea of Aceptology.

Which realities would you like to change?

If I want to change reality, it's because I haven't accepted it. For example, wanting to change everything happening around us, changing people, social structures, addressing all issues of injustice, solving other people's problems... that's our first struggle because we can't change the environment. And as long as I haven't accepted it, I haven't understood what it's teaching me. In other words, I'm not making use of what reality is showing me in correspondence with my inner self, learning from it without passing judgment on anyone.

If I accept it, I'd realize that what I need to change is something within me to align with the Universe's Order; that's the spiritual work.

I can fight in two ways: against what's happening in my life or against what I wish would happen. The idea is not to fight against anything, neither against what they do nor against what you would like to happen.

What we do is what corresponds to us. Enjoy it. Don't complain about it. Don't fight it. And for the things you can't do, it's because they don't correspond to you, so don't suffer or fight against them.

Until I understand that I lack the ability to disorganize the Universe or "organize" it, and that I have the capacity to flow with the existing order in the Universe ... until I understand that, the struggle will be endless, and so will suffering and conflict.

The simplest way to get out of conflict and struggle is to understand that the Universe is a Perfect Order governed by God and the Masters, not by the disciples or students... not by the children that we are. What children do is learn from the Universe; we don't govern it. That is the fundamental principle.

Jesus of Nazareth tells us in the Bible: **"You see the mote in your neighbor's eye but do not see the beam in your own."**

He speaks of the **mote and the beam**, where the problem in others always seems smaller than our own. When I feel upset with someone, for any reason, I'm seeing a flaw in them, which affects me. But when I see a flaw in them, I must learn that they are my mirror, reflecting something I need to change within me, probably something much larger than their flaw: the beam within me is the inability to accept someone with a different behavior than mine. I want them to be like me. The beam is the limitation I have in accepting others. Their flaw is just a speck to me. The problem to be resolved is not theirs but mine.

Similarly, when faced with reality, the same thing happens: I get upset about something, but it's my limitation in dealing with that reality that's a significant issue I need to resolve. If I now enter the reality that corresponds to me, that is, I choose to look inward and change my mindset about the reality that upsets me, this is what's referred to as "the awakening of consciousness."

If I start having fewer relationship problems, meaning a more peaceful coexistence with others; if I begin to have fewer financial problems, meaning having the resources I need to live and do what I love in life; if I start enjoying better physical and mental health, and if I start feeling more comfortable with where I am and what I do, it's clear that these indicators are showing my spiritual growth and development.Therefore, learning this is quite a challenge. It's a lot of work because the entire system of our beliefs, accumulated in our subconscious mind, shapes our personality and human ego, doesn't allow us to accept reality. As a result, we resist it. We resist people, structures, behaviors, and destinies. The more resistance I show, the more strength I give them, which leads to more opposition, conflict, and problems.

One possible solution is the practice of self-inquiry. We can become aware that every human being emits information through their vibration in the quantum field, and the Universe, along with everything in it, is organized based on this information.

Self-inquiry is a conscious observation in which I don't justify, I don't talk about others, I recognize that the other is my mirror, and I understand that what upsets me is in my shadow (according to C.G. Jung, perceiving the shadow is like looking in a mirror reflecting our personal unconscious).

We must learn from adversity because it has come to change or transform us. Therefore, the attitude to take in the face of a reality we can't change is one of acceptance or, in other words, surrender, not to be confused with resignation.

Surrender is an attitude in which I can't do anything more, so I decide to give this pain or problem to Universal Intelligence to accept the experience and learn from it. It's about accepting and then acting, to the best of my ability, but with a peaceful heart, with the learning that's meant for me to receive, and with emotional freedom.

There is no victimhood, no culprits because I am 100% responsible for everything that happens in my life. In one word: once reality is accepted, I must act without resentment.

The worst thing in life is living with resentment. It's like drinking a cup of poison and waiting for the other person to die.

Viktor Frankl said, "No one can take your place and suffer for you."

In the end, I understand that to be happy, I must learn to flow with life.

CHAPTER 5

THE EVOLUTIONARY STAGES OF THE HUMAN BEING
"Happiness is the natural state of children to whom the Kingdom belongs until they are corrupted and polluted by the stupidity of society and culture"
Anthony De Mello

In this chapter, we'll start talking about something really special: **the innocence of a child**. You see, kids are like these pure little beings, untouched by the often limiting web of beliefs that we adults get caught up in. They aren't responsible for the choices made on their behalf because, honestly, they don't have the info they need to make decisions or understand the consequences of their actions.

But here's the thing: that state of **INNOCENCE** doesn't last long in us humans. At around the age of 2, kids start absorbing the ancestral cultural info passed down through generations. They pick up ideologies, habits, customs, and behaviors based on the specific beliefs that shape their individual world.

In a nutshell, from the moment we're born, we get labeled with things like a name, a religion, certain beliefs, and ideas, among others. And it's highly likely that we carry childhood memories that influence the choices we make. The wrong thought patterns we develop shape our view of reality and how we relate to others, with all our fears, insecurities, and hang-ups.

For instance, if we were raised to think the world is a scary place, it's no wonder we might feel fear and insecurity in our everyday actions as adults. That's why it's crucial to reevaluate all those beliefs or ideas that were handed to us during childhood and no longer hold any meaning for us.

Living in fear, feeling disconnected, we've created a sort of mask, which we can call the Ego. Its main job? To protect us.

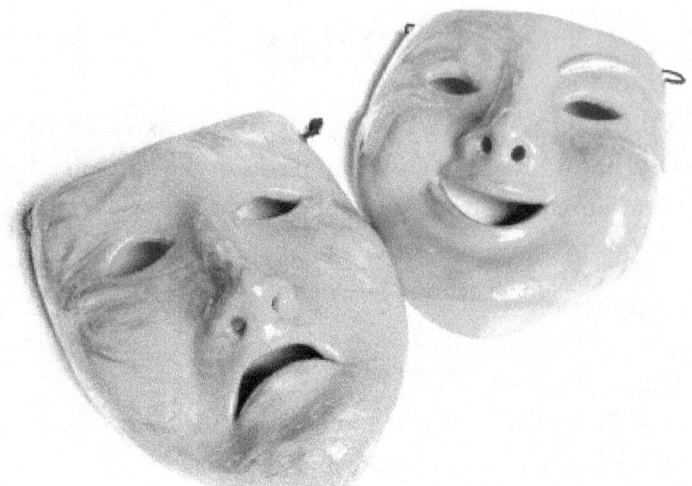

This phase of the self-transformation process is called **IGNORANCE**. It's the stage where us humans are completely swayed by ideas that haven't been confirmed as truth yet. We go about our lives and make choices based on limiting beliefs, which result in suffering, distress, loneliness, and dissatisfaction.

During this stage, we tend to think that problems and what we call conflicts come from external sources. So, we point fingers at the world, life, and others, blaming them for what we unconsciously generate in our own lives.

If we take a closer look at how we're put together and how we function, we'll find that we're mentally programmed with all sorts of assumptions about how the world should be, how we should be, and even what we should desire.

Society has made us dependent on success, approval, praise, and evaluation. When we don't get these, the suffering hits us hard. Many of us are hooked on seeking approval from others, but it's crucial to understand that our personal happiness doesn't rely on them.

So, **how do we go about changing things**? We often wish the other person would change to make us feel better, but that doesn't really cut it. It's us who need to change for things to change around us.

There's no clear explanation for all the suffering, evil, torture, destruction, and hunger in the world. There will never be an explanation for us because life itself is a mystery. That means the human mind, in all its rationality, can't make sense of it.

That's why we need to wake up and suddenly realize that the problem isn't reality; the problem is within ourselves.

At some point, we all get tired of butting heads with life. We grow weary of resisting situations and people who confront us with our inner discomfort. This fantastic moment is what we call the **SATURATION** phase.

When we realize the power of our ego to mess with our essence and decide not to let it take over our lives, that's when we start on the path to reconnect with our true selves. To do this, we might begin by questioning all those labels and beliefs that have been imposed on us since childhood.

Ask yourself and reflect honestly:

What would I be without the labels I've given myself?

Who would I become without these fears, flaws, and limitations?

Listen to that inner voice. It always tells you the truth! You can also dive into **meditation** to connect with your **essence** and leave the chaos of the Ego behind.

Taming our Ego is like breaking a wild horse – it takes tons of willpower, time, discipline, and persistence to get the results we desire.

The moment of saturation arrives when we experience the dark night of the soul and feel the need to examine ourselves, seeking new approaches that lead to different, more satisfying outcomes. For the first time, we take responsibility for our lives, actions, and the results we create. We realize that we've always reaped what we've sown, and if we want to harvest love, peace, and happiness, it starts with sowing conscious seeds filled with these qualities.

Spiritual growth can break down our socio-cultural barriers, revealing that life can be profoundly different. Through enthusiastic, continuous, and mindful training, we embrace the practice of trial and error, flowing with what works and produces the desired results. It's a shift from resisting life to challenging false beliefs.

The key here is persistence and focusing your attention on the right places.

Now, we come to the final stage, which we call **WISDOM**. In this phase, we clear our minds of limiting beliefs and make room for certainty, which always brings love, peace, and well-being. We return to purity, not the innocence of ignorance but a purity born from cleansing our minds of our own past ignorance. We operate from knowledge gained through personal experience, not mere theories or beliefs. Wisdom cannot be taught; it's the result of personal inner growth, requiring dedication, enthusiasm, and training.

We must be the masters of our own lives, fully aware of our decisions and the present moment. The unconscious mind tends to carry the baggage of the past, limiting our potential. Cleansing the unconscious paves the way for living in the present.

We need to break free from past beliefs and the projection of them into the future. Quit living on autopilot and start making your own choices.

If you're facing problems, it's because you're still asleep. Life itself isn't problematic; it's our own minds creating issues. Often, we worry about things that shouldn't concern us at all.

There's one ultimate need – the need for love. When someone discovers this, they are transformed. Miracles happen when we choose love. Love has the power to turn our lives into something beautiful. So, let love in!

CHAPTER 6

THE COSMIC AWAKENING

Just as individuals awaken their dormant consciousness, humanity as a whole is also evolving. It's what's known as the awakening of collective consciousness.

The world is changing...

American entrepreneur **Bill Gates** is known for his predictions. In 2015, the mogul had a pretty good idea of what the world would go through in 2020 when he stated that the next global catastrophe would be caused by "an epidemic"...

Now, **Bill Gates** says that in about five more years, a radical change is going to happen to our humanity! A new world order is going to set in among us... when we're already worn out from so much fear, so many insecurities, so much tension, so many conflicts, and so much submission to the priorities of those who govern us from the outside.

That would be around the year 2027...

Recently, **Bill Gates** has shared some new predictions that he believes will come true in the near future. After publishing a note on **GatesNotes**, his personal page, his predictions about processes that will become noticeable in the near future are now considered valuable insights into the future that's unfolding today with processes already in motion. Some of these, in the field of medicine, could turn out to be quite beneficial...

So why not take them into account?

Could he be a messenger, perhaps?

Bill Gates predicts that in the near future, we will have access to home medical diagnostics. Remote patient diagnosis will become much more accurate through devices that each one of us will have at home. Think of smartwatches with smart blood pressure monitors, for example. He also predicted that early diagnosis of Alzheimer's disease will reach a new level with widespread blood tests. According to him, there will be a significant breakthrough in this field in the next few years.

But what about those other technological advancements?

Bill Gates has foreseen what the next technological leap will be that will change humanity forever.

It's all about the use of **Artificial Intelligence (AI)**. We're in the early days of the autonomous era. In his words, we're about to reach a "tipping point." The technological breakthrough that will change the world, according to him, is the development of autonomous vehicles. "Self-driving cars will allow the driver to take their hands off the wheel and let the system drive in certain circumstances," he pointed out. Moreover, he believes this will be a game-changer for humanity, much like how personal computers revolutionized office work. It will prompt a rethinking of our transportation systems.

Another technological advancement that will change how we interact with others is the creation of a virtual world like the metaverse, as announced by **Mark Zuckerberg**. In his opinion, it will replace many online and in-person interactions. A life based on virtual avatars, remote work combined with virtual closeness, and an increasing part of life in this seemingly simulated world might appear dystopian but challenging to achieve.

However, **Bill Gates** thinks otherwise. He wrote, "The idea is that in the next two or three years, you'll use your avatar to meet people in a virtual space that replicates the feeling of being in a real room with them. To do that, you'll need VR glasses and motion-capture gloves to precisely capture your expressions, body language, and voice quality. Most people don't have these tools yet, which will slow down the adoption a bit."

We have to **WAKE UP!**

The message we can no longer evade is that the planet has reached a state of terminal crisis, and the only way out is through **LOVE** for others, our fellow humans, the same society that reflects us – in other words, ourselves – because...

We are **ALL** interconnected in this Universe created by a First Intelligence, which is our **GOD, DIVINE CREATOR, SOURCE, DIVINITY, ENERGY,** or whatever you want to call it...

The awakening of our sleepy conscience can be compared to the **experiment of the frog in a pot of water...**

When the frog **boils to death**, it's because it falls asleep slowly... as the water slowly heats up and is initially quite pleasant...

But **when the water temperature suddenly spikes, the frog jumps and saves itself!**

This is good advice for us to stay alert and remain connected with ourselves...

In the same vein, **we should consider crises as opportunities to stay awake and be always alert!**

If we reflect on everything we've been through at the beginning of this 21st century... starting with the terrorist threat in 2001, the financial crisis of 2008, which began with banks but ended up becoming public knowledge, with a massive fiscal crisis of government debt and terrible consequences reflected in the business world, leading to widespread job loss. Even in 2019, we were still dealing with its aftermath... and then we had to face yet another wave of a health crisis that affected **ALL OF HUMANITY in 2020...** And we know this is a process that won't stop, as one crisis will follow another.

But the difference now is that there's an evolution of collective consciousness with thousands of individuals advancing through various channels. People in this evolutionary journey will mobilize across distances to assist in awakening consciousness and showing solidarity to those in need.

THIS IS A HISTORIC MOMENT THAT WE DON'T HAVE TO LIVE IN FEAR...

There's a thirst for knowledge, for communication, for seeking and receiving information, for learning everything each one needs to continue evolving...

The time has come for all the masks of society to fall at a collective level. **Carl G. Jung** referred to masks as what we commonly know as persona, which is who we believe ourselves to be or how we want to appear to others, but it's not truly who we are.

J. Krishnamurti, in a conversation with his friend David Bohm, prompts us to reflect on the future of humanity when he says:

"[...] The unknown, the limitless cannot be captured by thought. Because thought itself is limited. Any action arising from limited thought (because knowledge is limited) will inevitably create conflict... Division itself creates insecurity."

"[...] If we consider the result of our world, dividing humanity geographically, into nationalities, ideological flags, borders, colors, social status, religions, and so on... If we feel that we are the rest of humanity, then our responsibility becomes immense. We have to participate: either we contribute to all the disorder or we stay out. That is to be at peace, ... starting to bring order to myself."

"All ideals are illusory."

"[...] It comes from our own perception ... from the activity of memory, which is limited...

Can humanity, mankind, live without conflict?

Can we have peace in this world?

[...] There is an activity beyond, untouched by thought, which is the highest form of Intelligence. We are all programmed, but that Intelligence has nothing to do with memory and knowledge."

"The world is me. I am the world. That is true meditation. We are inseparable."

"The consciousness of humanity has been divided by thought. All the problems humanity has now, psychologically, are the result of thought. We are following the same thought pattern over and over again, and thought will never solve any of these problems. So there is another kind of instrument, which is Intelligence."

"Without Love and Compassion, there is no Intelligence."

Thought versus Intelligence:

What is the future of humanity?

"As we can observe, it leads to DESTRUCTION: the outlook is very bleak, gloomy, and dangerous (...dystopian).

What about if you have children? Then education becomes extremely important.

Where nowadays education seems to be an accumulation of knowledge..."

"[...] Humanity is destroying nature, animals, farmlands, forests. Another problem is overpopulation. No one seems to care..."

"Does anyone care about the future of humanity? People only care about their own survival. That's why there are perpetual wars, perpetual insecurity. Those in power don't listen to anyone. They are creating more misery, more chaos, more danger."

As a human being, what is my responsibility?

The responsibility of those who see the problem and the responsibility of those who see nothing...

It's to start working for a better world."

To delve deeper and get to know the spiritual teacher **J. Krishnamurti** and the physicist **David Bohm,** who had already introduced the concept of the implicate and explicate order in the Universe, you can go to YouTube:**https://youtu.be/miMBSASO-Oo** - J. Krishnamurti and David Bohm The Future of Humanity 1st Conversation.

Reflections on Education

I would like to emphasize that all knowledge is useless without the ability to use it for questioning and experimenting, interacting with other disciplines and one's own environment. It's necessary for children to learn to think, to debate, to discover, to consult books and information, to organize data, and rework it with their own authenticity... to be little researchers!

In essence, going to school is also about... Learning to Learn![13]

We must enhance creativity, intelligence, intrinsic motivation in people and avoid the external social vacuum and discomfort that invades them. To do something that, potentially, requires the best of our human condition because we are all creative beings. That's what sets us apart from the rest of the animals. But our creativity is anesthetized! When have we been inspired to use it? ... in an industrial education system that teaches us to obey, to submit, to think in a certain way, until we reach adulthood completely conditioned, disconnected from ourselves and lost. Fortunately, neuroscience has shown that, thanks to the brain's neuroplasticity, certain neurons can be activated, and we can unlearn the programming instilled since childhood to introduce new habits, new skills, if we practice them and believe it's possible. That's the most revolutionary part: believing it's possible! Remember that...

If You Believe It, You Can Achieve It!

Allowing yourself to believe that you can't is letting others have mental control over you. So, the real revolution lies in changing education!

If we continue like this... these things will destroy the human race: politics without principles, progress without compassion, wealth without work, religion without fearlessness, and worship without consciousness.

If we can see that we are in the midst of the problem, each one of us must begin to work within ourselves for a better world. That is being at peace, starting to bring order to oneself.

Many ills afflict humanity from many fronts, but what's really important is to stay true to ourselves, by connecting in unity with that precious instrument that is our **First Intelligence, the Supraconsciousness.**

Having trust in Divine Providence is a unique source of love and not fearing the results because we are now completely detached from the ego.

The ego is the expression of our individuality; it's our identity card, which follows the dynamics of external materialism or the dual field, with a separation between self and other, as different entities. It operates with negative life dynamics of low frequencies, such as ignorance, victimhood, guilt, power. We see it, for example, with the war machine, synonymous with egomania, destruction, dominance, manipulation, death, to gain power and recognition.

Our **Ego loves to believe it's always right.** Furthermore, as a culture, we hold the false belief that whoever is right is the most powerful, the most intelligent, the most valuable, and the most successful; enough reasons to keep us in a constant power struggle, opinions, judgments, and beliefs that distance us from harmonious and peaceful coexistence.

So, who gets to be right?

The ego is convinced it knows it all, but it has no idea that it's permanently submerged in a dense tangle of limiting beliefs.

The one who is right is the one who can yield above their ego's whims... the one who yields in their beliefs, yields in their judgments, renounces imposing any idea on others, and is open to listening with curiosity and respect to others to expand their capacity to observe, their ability to learn to value their relationships, their ability to co-create with others a more harmonious, peaceful, happy, and unifying reality.

Love is the opposite of the ego.

If I don't understand or accept that in the Universe, everything has a purpose, that behind every situation, there is a lesson, and that wisdom is not about taking people out of their lesson but giving them the tools to make the most of it... then I will continue suffering indefinitely...

Don't give fish to the poor, teach them to fish!; Chinese Proverb.

Those who govern us, those who truly move the critical masses of the world, want people, that is, all of us, to think in certain ways, framed in a way of seeing and understanding the world, losing our ability to concentrate on our own spiritual being and, consequently, also our intelligence... and since everyone thinks the same, well, the world is just like that! And when there's someone who thinks differently, then they must be censored.

We're all sectarians; everyone has their way of seeing the world.

The world is a reflection of our perception, of our lives, of our beliefs... Everything is based on **THE ART OF OBSERVING...** because without an observer, without consciousness, there can be no manifestation.

The world is neither good nor bad; it depends on how each of us perceives it, and we must live well in it.

That's the world...

It all depends on the perception that I am having!

"Noise is not the Truth, noise is what men want to be true, and there is such a huge difference between those two things that it could kill you if you don't pay attention.". Patrick Ness, "The Knife of Never Letting Go", (2008).

"The noise is a man's thoughts without a filter. And without a filter, a man is nothing but chaos walking.

This is how **Chaos Walking** begins, the highly anticipated film adaptation of the eponymous trilogy written by **Patrick Ness**. The 2021 movie, directed by American filmmaker **Doug Liman** and based on a screenplay by **Patrick Ness and Christopher Ford**, is set in the New World, a planet inhabited by settlers and natives (the Spackle) and plagued by the Noise, a germ that only affects men, making all their thoughts audible and visible. This means that it's very hard to keep secrets unless you know how to control your **Noise (thoughts)**.

Returning to our reality, the economic system is specifically designed to redirect our attention toward a product or service, to create needs or program our minds to keep us entertained, **preventing us from thinking too much.**

Consider the fact that successful people don't watch the news or get caught up in the programming decided by the powerful because they show us the worst of the world. Instead, they focus on their own interests or try to solve their own problems. That's why each of us needs to focus on our own lives and take control to be part of the solution, not the problem.

It's hard to accept, but to improve our lives, each one of us should focus on the good, on quantum exchange, on the zero-point field. If everyone does their part, it would also improve the collective life.

We live in a world of constant fluctuations, where few things are characterized by stability. We're constantly asked to be flexible to adapt to changes in the way we relate to others, new social demands, professional revolutions, political, economic, and environmental events.

Amidst these dynamics, it's inevitable to experience some anxiety, insecurity, and fear. With this emotional state of vulnerability, it's easier to manipulate us with the strings of those who wield power.

We live in a permanent state of emergency, in a rapidly accelerating hurricane.

In the face of this, what should we do?

In **typhoons**, there's always a **place of salvation** where there's no wind, where the temperature is warm, like an oasis. This place is the **EYE OF THE HURRICANE,** where you can live with calm and joy.

The wise teach us to always choose the **MIDDLE PATH, to BREATHE AND MEDITATE IN THE HERE AND NOW.**

Within this framework, we're taught to **maintain Calm amidst Chaos,** to achieve composure and security amid this **liquid uncertainty.**

Who better than the celebrated philosopher **Zygmunt Bauman** can talk to us about the concept of **Liquid Society**? Over a decade ago, he used this term to describe a modernity of shifting values, variable social models and structures, and unstable realities. In this fragile and fluctuating context where it's very hard to commit to anything, the only truly solid things are our fears, which constitute a genuine paradox.

Fear arises when there is a conflict between what we desire and what we do, inevitably leading to tension due to discrepancies between the two. We must reflect on the extent to which we are aware that we are conditioned, controlled by programs that nest in our unconscious, and that our minds and thoughts are creating our reality based on our own judgments.

There's a famous Bible verse that says, **"with the measure you use, it will be measured to you."** Let's look at the world with a nonjudgmental mind, with the mind of a child, with humility, with innocence. Only in this way, with a mind free of prejudices, can we truly see the world without giving it more power. Because if I condemn the world, given that I am the one creating it moment by moment, I am condemning myself. Therefore, we must live in this world and observe it, but without passing judgment.

Tesla said, **"EVERY JUDGMENT IS A SELF-CONFESSED."**

I don't see things as they are but as I am.

I interpret reality through my perception, which is a product of projection.

That's why we're going to take care of the food for the mind: thoughts and words that cause our emotions, and we're not going to judge anyone but put ourselves in the other person's shoes.

We're going to become aware and accept, even when we perceive that we can't do anything more to change a certain situation, without expectations of how everyone would like things to be, without forcing anything but allowing the best option, the best possibility, to express itself in our lives. We'll let that **Prime Intelligence, the Universe, God…** decide what's best for each of us because as far as we're concerned, we have no idea!

It's like a drop in the ocean within the ocean itself. If we become quantum and enter a drop in the ocean, we would see the whole ocean. **Rumi**, the 13th-century Sufi master, said, **"Only one in a million understands that a drop of the ocean contains the entire ocean."**

The key to evolution is uniting the three consciousnesses and aligning the mind with the heart. The supraconscious vibrates at a high frequency because it performs its functions perfectly, drawing its energy from the wisdom accumulated in our Higher Self. Intuition is its language. Intuition is our inner voice that will always guide us toward the most perfect path.

If we integrate our mind, it will operate only with intuitive data coming from our Higher Self. In summary, Supraconsciousness, Infraconsciousness, and Consciousness are a single whole that's often disintegrated in most people. Ancient philosophers often represented this reality with the metaphor of the dismembered God, like a shattered mirror where everything, although of the same nature, is separated.

Master **Gerardo Schmedling** teaches us that: **"Regardless of whether I do or do not exist, nothing in the Universe will stop functioning as it should..."**

"I choose to declare myself in a state of peace and love and not be a part of defenses, violence, or aggression of any kind... He reminds us that **"everyone generates their own correspondence within the Universe..."** He tells us that: **"As long as I believe I can make someone happy or improve someone's life, I'm already wrong... because it's the same as if I believed someone could do that for me...**

What we can do is share values." "[...] If I have love in my heart, the capacity to serve, the capacity to accept, I can share that with another, but I can't give them what they are not capable of receiving; this is where the wisdom of the Universe lies, and this is where Acceptology begins:

[...] I am just a tiny part of every form. My form is temporary... as it is also eternal. It's temporary in the sense that my body has a lifespan, and it's eternal in the sense that the information that originated it, originates from God and therefore will never disappear. As long as I have concerns or sufferings, I am not loving, and I don't have sufferings when I understand the function of a human being for themselves...

"This is to LEARN two things: TO BE HAPPY AND TO LOVE."

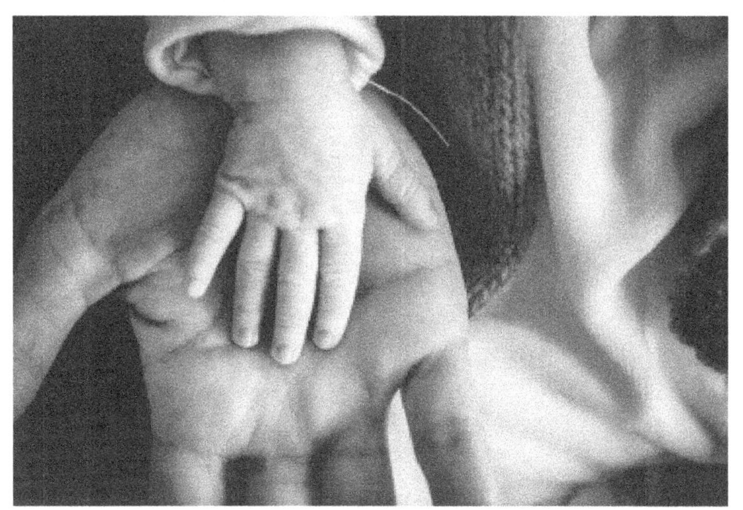

CONCLUSION

WE HUMAN BEINGS ARE APPEARANCE AND ESSENCE

Unfortunately, present-day humanity often loses sight of this fact, as it becomes too attached to the material, identifying primarily with its physical, ephemeral, and transitory aspect while neglecting or not paying attention to its spiritual, eternal, and immortal aspect.

For those individuals who are awakening to this sleepy conscience, who are beginning to perceive that higher vibration of the eternal within them, it is essential to take a more decisive step to integrate it into their everyday lives. It shouldn't be just an intellectual understanding that there is something more.

Throughout the process of evolution, it should lead us not only to become aware of all this but also to live in coherence and consistency so that this eternal **ESSENCE** we are gradually takes conscious command of our lives. However, this step is not easy, as we are continually distracted by consumerism, material possessions, and selfishness.

If we don't like what's happening in the world today, let's begin by **AWAK-ENING OUR SLEEPY CONSCIENCE** and allowing ourselves to be enveloped by that **UNIVERSAL CONSCIOUSNESS** to once again **become a part of the whole and the whole itself.**

If we want to create a new world, we have to embody it within ourselves, transmute it into our being and better interaction with others, thus generating a new vibration that is coherent and compatible with this new world we are, for it to materialize: Living in the here and now. Living in the eternal present.

Consciousness evolves like the train of life, where every person has an opportunity, hope, and a place to grow, to progress.

There is a good destiny for everyone, tailored to each person's measure.

The train moves towards its destination on two rails: utopia and dystopia.

Where is our freedom of choice?

Living consciously is the best decision we can make. Be participant observers: observe and listen to ourselves; understand and forgive ourselves; disidentify to discover the self, to be at peace.

The key to living consciously is to focus on what we think and what we feel, to know what we decide, and the attitude with which we act. This way, we will begin to take control of our lives and be our own masters.

Let's not allow ourselves to be as vulnerable as puppets, being pulled from one side to another, letting events and people tell us how to feel. Push a button to make us depressed? Do people really like that? But if we refuse to identify with those puppets, most of our worries would cease.

Let's not allow the powerful of the world to strip us of our **ESSENCE**...

Our Essence is what makes us feel connected, makes us feel united with Creation and its Origin, merging into One with the Whole, the Consciousness of Unity.

Anthony de Mello, in his book **"Awareness"**[14], said: **"If you could understand this, you would discover the secret of awakening. You would be happy forever. You will never be unhappy again. Nothing could ever hurt you. I mean it: nothing. It's like when black paint is spilled into the air; the air remains uncontaminated. You can never paint the air black. No matter what happens to you, you remain uncontaminated. You remain in peace."**

I leave you with this quote from **Anthony de Mello** to conclude this book and reflect:

"You can't paint the air black... you can't contaminate it, and you remain in peace..."

◈ THANK YOU ◈

Ana María Pepi

...To be continued

[1] Acceptology & You Are the Best of Yourself & Parenting School. Soft Cover. August 5, 2014. (Spanish edition) Gerardo Schmedling (Author).

[2] A Course in Miracles (Spanish Edition) Hardcover. 1 September 2007. Dr. Helen Schucman (Author) Publisher: Foundation for Inner Peace.

[3] Letters to Claudia (Spanish Edition) Softcover. 1 July 2010. Spanish Edition by Jorge Bucay (Author).Editorial: Del Nuevo Extremo; First Edition.

[4] Chaos Walking Series. The Knife of Never Letting Go (Book 1). Patrick Ness (Author), published by Walker Books on 5 May 2008.

[5] In the J. A. Bayonas's film, "A Monster Calls", the boy Connor, in his recurring 00:07 nightmare suffers for his mother who is dying, but he can't accept that reality... He doesn't want to let her go. On one hand, he wanted all to be over, but at the same time he didn't want it...because it would mean losing her....

His mother used to tell him that he would be better off, because that's what Connor wanted to happen... (those were his white lies) But the harsh reality was another one....

[6] El Camino de la Felicidad. (The Way to Happiness) Softcover – February 6, 2004. Spanish edition. Jorge Bucay (Author). Editorial: GRIJALBO; 2nd edition.

[7] In the J. A. Bayonas's film, "A Monster Calls", the Monster asks Connor to tell him the 4th story, which is his own: THE TRUTH. Now is the time to tell YOUR TRUTH, Connor. It will kill you not to tell the TRUTH... and then Connor tells him that at the end of his nightmare he finally releases his mother... At last, you have said it! You have been BRAVE. When Connor ACCEPTS THE REALITY, he is at peace...

Jesus of Nazareth said, "The TRUTH will set you FREE..."

[8] "Los Colores del Arcoiris. Maravillosa Capacidad de Asombro" (The Colors of the Rainbow. Wonderful Capacity for Amazement), by Mariah Carreon. Spanish edition, 2022. Bestseller book translated into Italian by Ana Maria Pepi.

[9] 20 Pasos hacia Adelante (20 Steps Forward). Softcover – 23 February 2012. Spanish edition. Jorge Bucay (Author). Edtorial: RBA libros.

[10] The Book of Spirits (Spanish Edition) Hardcover. 1 April 2021. Spanish Edition by Allan Kardec (uthor), Jesús Arroyo Cruz (Editor).

[11] "A 50 años del golpe militar en Chile: y a 35 años de que la alegría no llegó", by bestselling author Nelson Carrizo, El Poeta Minero, 2023. Book translated into Italian by Ana María Pepi.

[12] Claim Your Fortune!: The Initiates Saga. Volume 3, written by bestselling author Jack Baker, 2023

[13] LEARNING Volume 1: ABSOLUTE POWER.
The Art of Learning How to Do it.

[14] Awareness: The Perils and Opportunities of Reality (1990) by Anthony De Mello (Author 1931-1987 India).

Don't miss out!

Visit the website below and you can sign up to receive emails whenever Ana María Pepi publishes a new book. There's no charge and no obligation.

https://books2read.com/r/B-A-CNIEB-XXKYC

Connecting independent readers to independent writers.

Did you love *Learning Volume 2: Wake up Your Sleepy Conscience. The Art of Learning to Accept Reality and Choosing How to Live It.*? Then you should read *Learning: Absolute Power. The Art of Learning How to Do it.*[1] by Ana María Pepi!

Learning How To Do It is the Absolute Power that the human being possesses to obtain everything that is proposed in life.We are made of body and soul, therefore there is no success if we do not put emotion to the things we undertake every day.The mind can do everything with its Absolute Power.On the physical plane, we have at our disposal an internal computer, super powerful, which is our brain, although we do not always consider it with the importance it deserves! In this book we will learn how to treat it well so that it performs at the highest level, because being a muscle, we have to train it as we do with our body.On the spiritual plane, we have the soul, the emotions that push us to do everything in life!They are those vibrations that change our mood, which in the metaphysical plane is everything that we do not see but

---

1. https://books2read.com/u/3L52d5

2. https://books2read.com/u/3L52d5

that we feel inside us, and that we know with the name of intuitions.In school they teach us the subjects we have to study, but they do NOT teach us how to do it!This book is an invitation to make a journey of transformation and growth to become new and better people, to achieve the results you have set for yourself in life, whether in the area of money, health or love.In this book you will find a lot of valuable information and many tips, secrets and methods for you to put your Absolute Power into practice!Learning to Learn How to succeed in life....Learning to Learn How to stay motivated and not lose focus on what you're doing...Learning to Learn How to study in a more effective way and obtain, thanks to your Absolute Power, greater results...Learning to Learn How to read faster and increase your knowledge to the highest degree to reach your goals before others...Learning to Learn How to memorize names, speeches and studies in an easier, more effective and entertaining way...Learning to Learn How to speak a foreign language effortlessly while having fun...All this and much more in the pages of this book, waiting for you to make the most of your Absolute Power to transform yourself from what you are today into what you can be tomorrow.This book does not pretend to be neither scientific nor miraculous, it has only the recipe to prepare you every day to be the best version of yourself, to grow and never stop learning.It is a recipe prepared from the heart. Whether you practice it or discard it, it's up to you!LEARNING TO LEARN is that curious impulse that leads you to investigate and be self-taught.LEARN TO LEARN is the greatest booster for your personal growth and development!LEARN TO LEARN is the most awesome and powerful ability you have at your disposal! It is your Absolute Power!You can do it all!Happy Journey!

Also by Ana María Pepi

LEARNING

Learning Volume 2: Wake up Your Sleepy Conscience. The Art of Learning to Accept Reality and Choosing How to Live It.

Standalone

Aprendiendo: Poder Absoluto. El Arte de Aprender CóMo se Hace
Imparando: Potere Assoluto. L'Arte di Imparare Come si Fa
Learning: Absolute Power. The Art of Learning How to Do it.
Aprendiendo Tomo 2: Despierta tu Conciencia Dormida. El Arte de Aceptar la Realidad y Elegir Cómo Vivirla
Imparando Volume 2: Risveglia la tua Coscienza Dormiente. L'Arte di Imparare ad Accettare la Realtà E Scegliere Come Viverla

About the Author

I am Ana Maria Pepi, Italian-Argentinean. I was born in the Province of Mendoza, the land of sun and good wine, very near to the Andes Mountains.My parents were Italian, originally from "Le Marche", a region famous in the world for its excellence in the production of "Made in Italy" footwear. In this beautiful place, on the coast of the Adriatic Sea, is where I currently live.I am Mendocina and I am Marchigiana.In Argentina, after obtaining the Diploma in Accounting, at the age of 17, I entered the National University of Cuyo, Faculty of Philosophy and Letters, to study English Language and Literature to be an English Teacher. But, After moving to Italy, I graduated at Macerata University in Modern Foreign Languages and Literatures: English and Spanish.And so, I am trilingual.I am a curious and optimistic soul, my great passion is to constantly learn new things, explore new worlds whether in reading or traveling.Learning how things are done is an emotional journey for curious and observant people who are hungry to know in order to be more productive and happy.My dominant question is how can I be more useful and put myself at the service of others.Eureka! The best way to learn is to teach! because...."By teaching we learn." Lucius Annaeus Seneca.With this binomial I can satisfy my 2 greatest passions, learning and teaching!My purpose with this book is to contribute with my grain of sand, to leave a legacy, to inspire the curious like me, with what I have read and learned so far... to improve our level of life in all its senses, money, health and love, making better decisions!The best reward for me is knowing that with this book I can help a great number of people to realize their dreams....Miracles are not expected, they are created!